ALL THUMBS

Guide to Home Energy Savings

Other All Thumbs Guides

Home Wiring
Home Plumbing
Painting, Wallpapering, and Stenciling
Repairing Major Home Appliances
VCRs

Guide to
Home Energy
Savings

Robert W. Wood
Illustrations by Steve Hoeft

TAB | **TAB BOOKS**
Blue Ridge Summit, PA

FIRST EDITION
FIRST PRINTING

Library of Congress Cataloging-in-Publication Data

Wood, Robert W. 1933-
    Home energy savings / by Robert W. Wood
        p.   cm.
    Includes index.
    ISBN 0-8306-4164-5 (pbk.)
1. Dwellings--Energy conservation. I. Title
TJ163.5.D86W66   1992   92-15735
644--dc20   CIP

Acquisitions editor: Kimberly Tabor
Editorial team: Susan D. Wahlman, Editor
               Stacey Spurlock, Indexer
Production team: Katherine G. Brown, Director of Production
                 Wanda S. Ditch, Layout
                 Susan E. Hansford, Typesetting
Design team: Jaclyn J. Boone, Designer
             Brian Allison, Associate Designer
Cover design: Lori E. Schlosser
Cover illustration: Denny Bond, East Petersburg, Pa.
Cartoon caricature: Michael Malle, Pittsburgh, Pa.   ATS

The All Thumbs Guarantee

TAB Books/McGraw-Hill guarantees that you will be able to follow every step of each project in this book, from beginning to end, or you will receive your money back. If you are unable to follow the All Thumbs steps, return this book, your store receipt, and a brief explanation to:

All Thumbs
P.O. Box 581
Blue Ridge Summit, PA 17214-9998

About the Binding

This and every All Thumbs book has a special lay-flat binding. To take full advantage of this binding, open the book to any page and run your finger along the spine, pressing down as you do so; the book will stay open at the page you've selected.

The lay-flat binding is designed to withstand constant use. Unlike regular book bindings, the spine will not weaken or crack when you press down on the spine to keep the book open.

Contents

Preface

A collection of books about do-it-yourself home repair and improvement, the All Thumbs series was created not for the skilled jack-of-all-trades, but for the average homeowner. If your familiarity with the various systems in the home is minimal, or your budget doesn't keep pace with today's climbing costs, this series is tailor-made for you.

Several different types of professional contractors are required to construct even the smallest home. Carpenters build the framework, plumbers install the pipes, and electricians complete the wiring. Few people can do it all. The necessary skills often require years to master. The professional works quickly and efficiently and depends on a large volume of work to survive. Because service calls are time-consuming, often requiring more travel time than actual labor, they can be expensive. The All Thumbs series saves you time and money by showing you how to make most common repairs yourself.

The guides cover topics such as home wiring; plumbing; painting, stenciling, and wallpapering; repairing major appliances; and cutting home energy costs, to name a few. Copiously illustrated, each book details the procedures in an easy-to-follow, step-by-step format, making many repairs and home improvements well within the ability of nearly any homeowner.

Introduction

Y ou only have to look at your monthly utility bills to know that the cost of energy is rising and taking a much bigger bite out of the household budget. Any homeowner can reduce these direct costs in a few simple and usually inexpensive steps. Not only will these steps take the strain off your bank account, they will help with the biggest environmental problems associated with the production of energy and its use: air pollution, acid rain, and global warming. The nice part about cutting home energy costs is that you also help save the environment.

This book tells you how to inspect your home for areas that waste energy, such as air leaks and inadequate insulation. Then, step-by-step instructions show you how to seal doors and windows and install insulating materials. Next, you'll learn ways to save water and electricity, followed by ways to use heating and cooling systems most efficiently. One chapter explains how to improve air circulation and save energy by installing a ceiling fan, attic fan, or roof turbine. The last chapter explains how you can use major appliances most efficiently.

The tools and materials lists in each chapter include everything you need if you are going to do all of the projects in that chapter . Be sure to read the steps first to determine exactly what you want to do. Then refer back to the tools and materials list to see what you need to buy.

All of the steps in this book can be taken by almost anyone, but even if you only do a few of them, not only should you save money on your energy bills, but you'll also feel good about doing your part for the environment.

CHAPTER ONE

Inspecting Your Home

Some utility companies offer free energy inspections, or you can do your own. The point to remember is a basic law of physics: heat moves toward cold. In winter the heated air in your home tries to move to the cold outside, and in the summer the hot air outside tries to get into the coolness of your home. The harder your heating or cooling system has to work to overcome this law, the higher your utility bills. Installing adequate insulation and sealing air leaks go a long way to reduce this transfer of energy, but first you need to know where to look. Make a list of any places that need attention.

Tools & Materials
- ❏ Pencil and paper
- ❏ Tape measure or ruler
- ❏ Flashlight
- ❏ Ladder

Step 1-1. Checking outlets.

This test works best on a windy day. Hold your hand close to each switch plate and receptacle, particularly on the outside walls. You might be surprised to find drafts coming from several outlets.

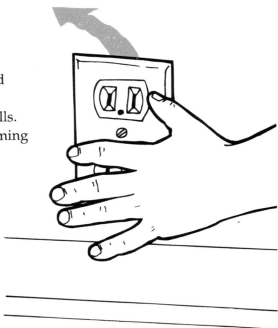

Step 1-2.
Checking baseboards.

Run your hand along the baseboard to check for drafts where the baseboard meets the floor and where it meets the wall.

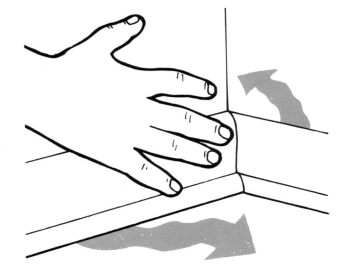

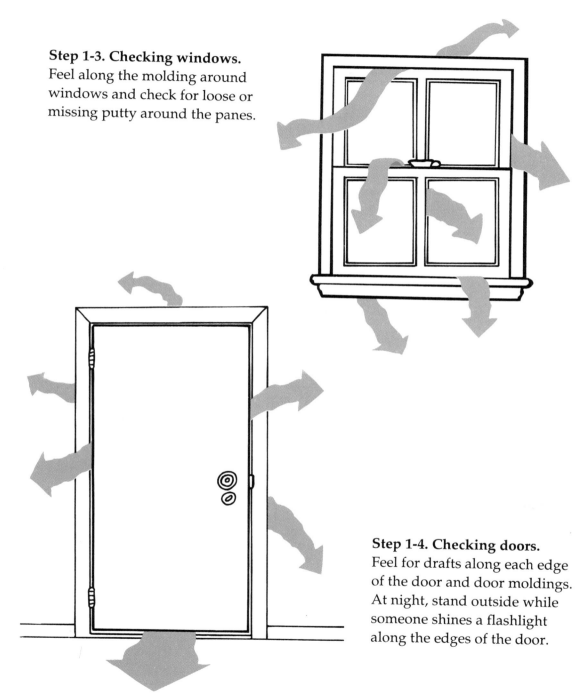

Step 1-3. Checking windows.
Feel along the molding around windows and check for loose or missing putty around the panes.

Step 1-4. Checking doors.
Feel for drafts along each edge of the door and door moldings. At night, stand outside while someone shines a flashlight along the edges of the door.

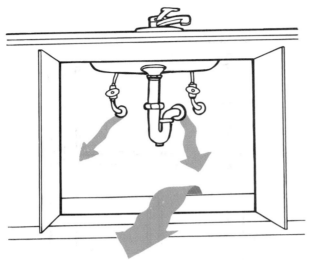

Step 1-5.
Checking plumbing outlets.
Use the flashlight to check under the sinks for gaps where the pipes enter the walls. Then feel for any drafts.

Step 1-6.
Checking fireplaces.
Hold your hand inside the opening in the fireplace to check for drafts. The damper could be open or the cleanout door (if you have one) might not be closed properly. Now check for drafts along the edges where the wall and ceiling meet the fireplace.

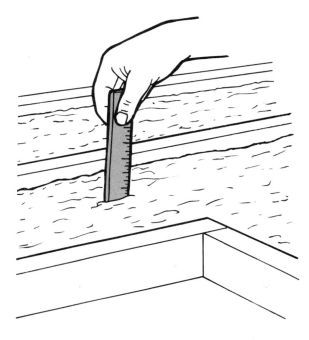

Step 1-7.
Checking the attic insulation.
Feel for any drafts around the access hatch. Then open the hatch and climb up into the attic. If the attic has no floor, measure the depth of the insulation and write it down for later use.

Step 1-8.
Checking the attic for gaps and fire hazards.
Notice whether all nooks are filled and the areas around vent pipes are covered. Make sure that all recessed light fixtures and exhaust fans have a 3-inch uninsulated space around them. The space between a chimney and any wood framing should be filled with a noncombustible material such as sheet metal sealed with silicone caulk.

3-inch gap

Step 1-9. Checking a ventilated crawl space.

If you have a ventilated crawl space, measure the thickness of the insulation under the floor and write it down for later use. Check for drafts around any openings where electrical cables and plumbing go through the floor.

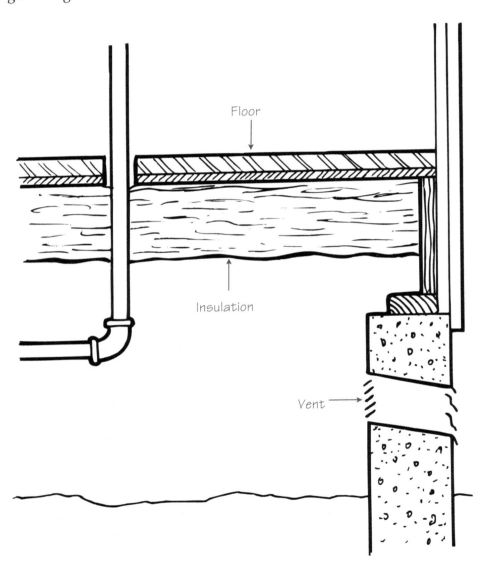

Step 1-10. Checking the basement.
Look for drafts along outside walls where the
floor sits on top of the basement walls.

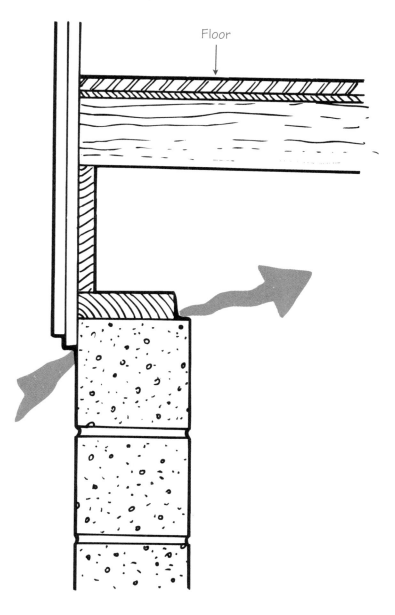

Floor

Step 1-11. Checking a slab floor.

Go outside and check for drafts where the walls sit on top of the foundation. Stopping drafts with caulking and weatherstripping is one of the easiest ways to save home energy costs. Check with your paint or building-supply dealer for the best type of caulking for your specific needs. Generally, oil-based caulking is the least expensive, but it's not too durable. Acrylic latex is the easiest to use, cleans up with water, and can be painted immediately with latex paint. Silicone caulk is the most expensive and lasts the longest. It does not take paint well; however, it is available in various colors. Use a flexible foam, sold in long rolls, to fill larger (1/4 inch or more) cracks before caulking.

CHAPTER TWO

Sealing Doors

Your home's exterior doors probably already have some form of weatherstripping. If you found drafts during your inspection, make sure the door closes firmly and has no play after it is closed. Try adjusting the existing weatherstripping before you replace it. If the weatherstripping is spring metal, try bending it back away from the doorway with a putty knife. If the door has a door sweep, the sweep probably has oblong screw slots. Loosen the screws and reposition the sweep closer to the floor. Most thresholds have a replaceable vinyl gasket. Pry a damaged one out with a screwdriver and take it with you to a hardware store to buy a replacement. Cut the new one to fit and pry it into the slots in the threshold with the screwdriver.

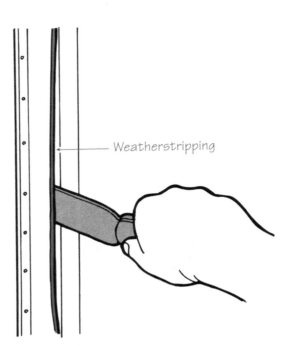

Bend spring-metal weatherstripping back into place with a putty knife.

Weatherstripping

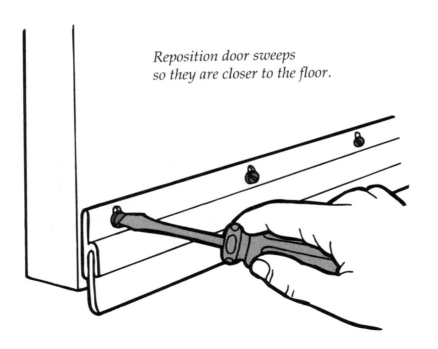

Reposition door sweeps so they are closer to the floor.

Replace damaged vinyl gaskets in thresholds.

Tools & Materials

- ❑ Tape measure
- ❑ Weatherstripping
- ❑ Utility knife or heavy scissors
- ❑ Hammer and nails or screwdriver and screws
- ❑ Tin snips
- ❑ Putty knife
- ❑ Hacksaw
- ❑ Power saw
- ❑ Paintbrush
- ❑ Dry cloth
- ❑ Caulking gun
- ❑ Good-quality flexible caulking
- ❑ Door sweep, door shoe, or threshold

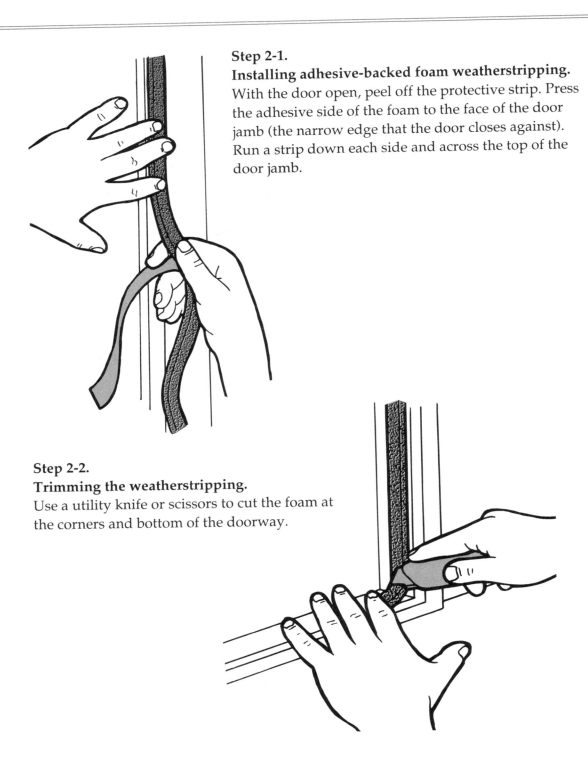

Step 2-1.
Installing adhesive-backed foam weatherstripping.
With the door open, peel off the protective strip. Press the adhesive side of the foam to the face of the door jamb (the narrow edge that the door closes against). Run a strip down each side and across the top of the door jamb.

Step 2-2.
Trimming the weatherstripping.
Use a utility knife or scissors to cut the foam at the corners and bottom of the doorway.

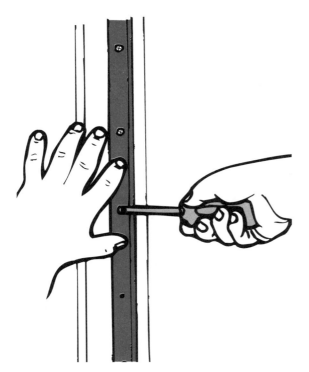

Step 2-3.
Buying rolled-vinyl,
aluminum-backed weatherstripping.
The metal backing is predrilled for nails or screws. It might have holes or slots. Slots allow you to adjust the strips. Over time, however, strips with slots will be pushed out of position, and after several adjustments, the screws won't hold. Try to get the metal strips with holes, not slots. Cut a strip to fit from the top of the doorway to the bottom.

Step 2-4.
Installing vinyl weatherstripping.
Close the door and, from the outside, hold the strip against the doorstop. Position the strip so that the vinyl fits snugly against the door. Fasten the strip in place with nails or screws. The process is easier if you start the screw, then open the door, and finish driving the screw into place. Repeat the steps for the top and the hinge side.

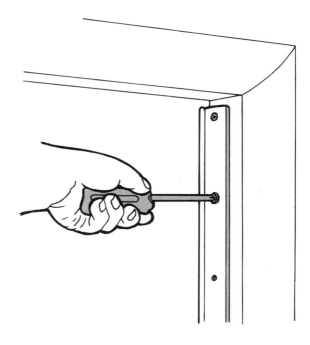

Step 2-5.
Cutting spring-metal weatherstripping.
Use tin snips to cut one strip to fit across the top of the
doorway. Then cut strips to fit each side. The strip
that fits on the side with the door latch should
be cut into segments so that it does not cover
the striker plates for the door latch and
dead bolt.

Step 2-6.
Weatherstripping the striker plates.
A short, narrow strip is provided with the
weatherstripping to fit inside the wider strip,
behind the striker plate.

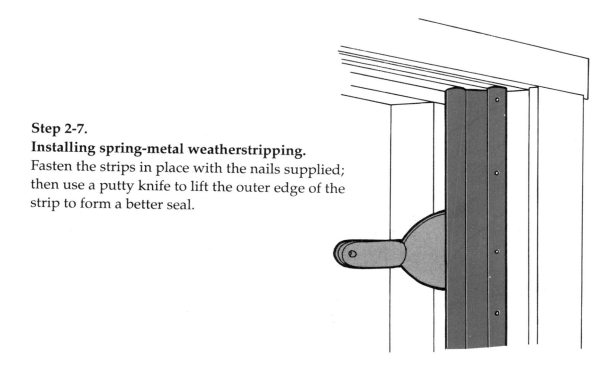

Step 2-7.
Installing spring-metal weatherstripping.
Fasten the strips in place with the nails supplied;
then use a putty knife to lift the outer edge of the
strip to form a better seal.

Step 2-8.
Installing a door sweep.
A door sweep is a one-piece strip
of metal-reinforced rubber or vinyl
that fits along the lower edge of the
door. Use the hacksaw to cut the
sweep to fit about 1/16 inch from
each edge of the door.

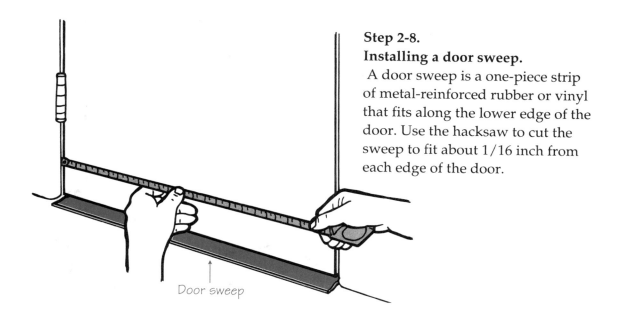

Door sweep

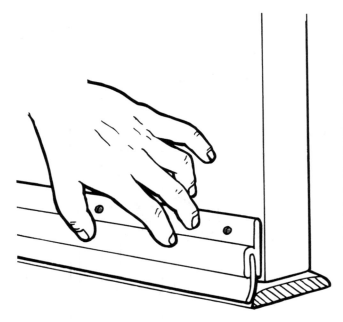

Step 2-9.
Aligning the door sweep.
Align the sweep along the lower edge of the door on the inside of the room. Position it so that the bottom edge of the sweep seals the threshold but still allows the door to open easily. Mark the screw holes to keep the sweep aligned properly.

Step 2-10. Mounting the sweep.
Fasten the sweep in place with screws. This type of sweep works well if the door opens over a hard-surfaced floor. Spring-loaded sweeps that lift automatically are available for carpeted floors.

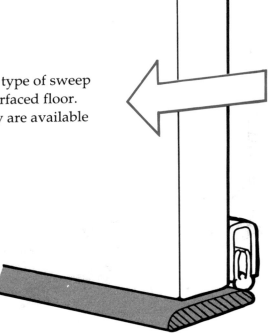

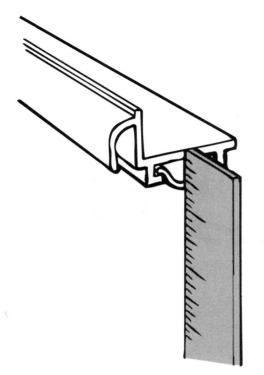

Step 2-11. Installing a door shoe.

A door shoe works like a door sweep except it is attached to the bottom of the door and is less conspicuous. However, you might have to shorten the door. Measure the height of the shoe, allowing for the gasket that compresses against the threshold, to determine how much to trim off the door. *Note:* If you have a metal door, you'll probably need to have a carpenter modify the door frame.

Step 2-12. Marking the door.

Remove the door and mark the cut on both sides of the door with a pencil. Use a utility knife to cut along the mark to prevent splintering when you use the power saw.

Step 2-13. Cutting the door.

Be sure to read and follow the manufacturer's safety instructions for using your power saw. Then use the saw to trim the measured amount off the bottom of the door. Use the hacksaw to cut the door shoe to fit the width of the door.

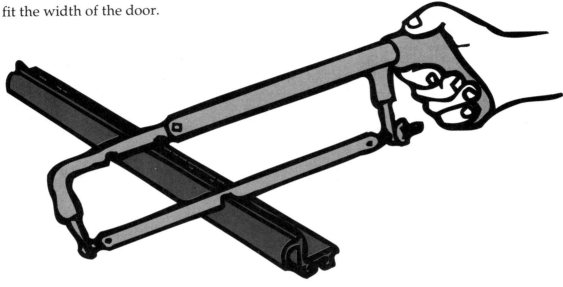

Step 2-14.
Mounting the shoe.

Slide the gasket out of the base of the shoe and fasten the base to the bottom of the door with screws. Reinstall the gasket and rehang the door.

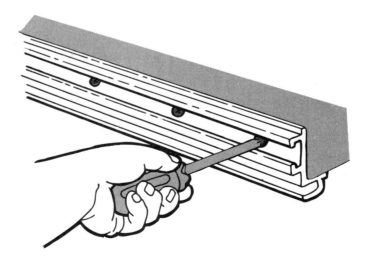

Step 2-15.
Installing a threshold.

Interlocking thresholds are available, but they are difficult to install. A simpler threshold has a vinyl gasket. The bottom of the door might have to be trimmed, but this time you need approximately an 1/8-inch bevel to seal against the gasket.

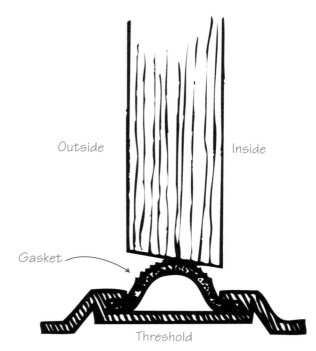

Outside   Inside

Gasket

Threshold

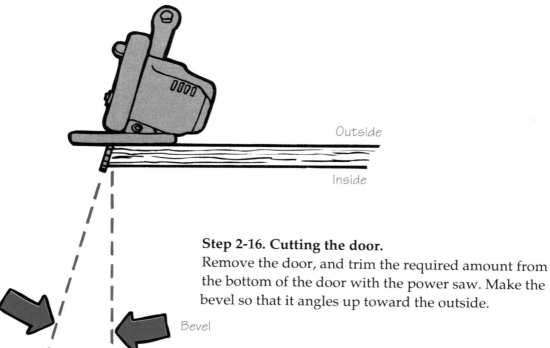

Outside

Inside

Bevel

Step 2-16. Cutting the door.

Remove the door, and trim the required amount from the bottom of the door with the power saw. Make the bevel so that it angles up toward the outside.

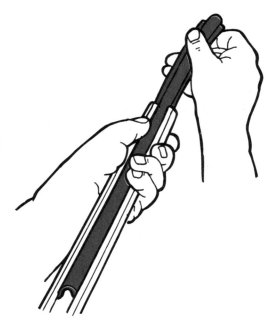

Step 2-17. Mounting the threshold.
Use the hacksaw to cut the threshold to fit the opening in the doorway. Slide out the gasket and install the metal base with screws. Reinstall the gasket.

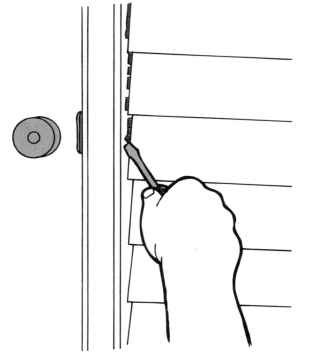

**Step 2-18.
Caulking the door frame.**
Caulk the joints where the door frame meets the siding. First remove any flecked paint or caulking along the joint with the tip of a screwdriver. Brush off any dust with a dry paintbrush.

Step 2-19.
Opening the caulking tube.
Open the tube of caulking by slicing off the tip of the nozzle at an angle. Cut a small opening for a narrow bead, a bigger opening for a wider bead.

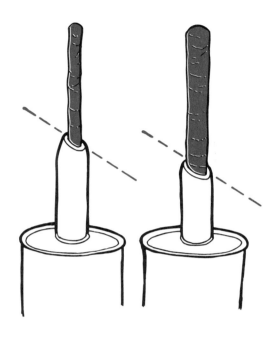

Step 2-20.
Applying the caulking.
Hold the point of the tube to the joint so that the caulking is forced deep into the crack. Apply smooth, steady pressure to get an even bead. Make sure the bead overlaps both edges for a tight seal. Remove any excess with your fingertip or a dry cloth.

CHAPTER THREE

Sealing Windows

Sealing windows is an easy project that can be accomplished with minimal tools and expense. Window weatherstripping is sold in kits—one for each window—or in lengths by the running foot. In either case, you have to measure the windows to know how much weatherstripping you need. The type of weatherstripping you choose depends on the kind of windows you have, either wood or aluminum. You can use spring-metal or rolled-vinyl weatherstripping on wood windows. Foam rubber with adhesive backing can be applied to casement windows. With aluminum windows, your options are normally limited to applying caulking or installing insulated window shades or blinds. You also can install one of two types of storm windows—a thin plastic film that you attach to the inside or outside of the window, or a removable rigid acrylic or glass pane installed by a contractor.

Tools & Materials

- ❏ Tape measure
- ❏ Weatherstripping
- ❏ Tin snips
- ❏ Hammer and nails
- ❏ Tacks
- ❏ Nail set
- ❏ Utility knife
- ❏ 6-mil polyethylene plastic
- ❏ ¼ -×-1¼ -inch wood slats
- ❏ Screwdriver
- ❏ Paintbrush
- ❏ Caulking gun and caulking
- ❏ Dry cloth

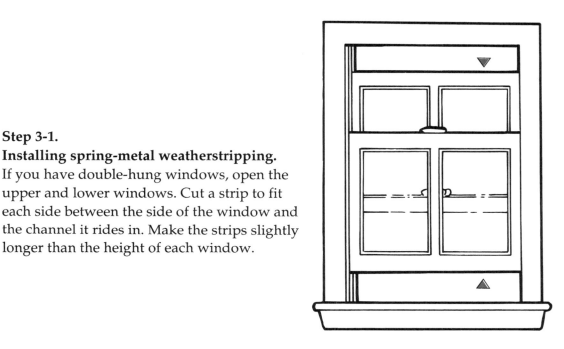

Step 3-1.
Installing spring-metal weatherstripping.
If you have double-hung windows, open the
upper and lower windows. Cut a strip to fit
each side between the side of the window and
the channel it rides in. Make the strips slightly
longer than the height of each window.

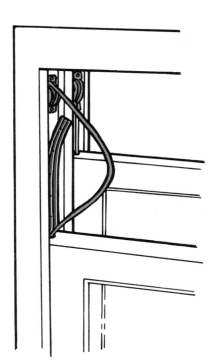

Step 3-2.
Fitting the weatherstripping.
Cut out a section so that you don't cover the pulleys
in the upper channels. Tack the strips in the channels
so that the edge with the nail holes points inward,
toward the inside of the house.

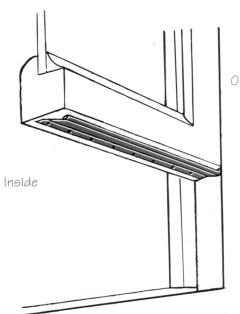

Outside

Inside

Step 3-3.
Installing strips on top and bottom rails.
Cut strips to fit the full width of the bottom of the lower window and the top of the upper window. Tack them in place, with the nail edge inward, along the top of the upper window and the bottom of the lower window.

Step 3-4.
Installing the strip between the upper and lower windows.
Cut a strip to fit the full width of the bottom part of the upper window. Tack it in place on the inside part of the upper window with the nail edge up. Countersink the nails slightly so they don't rub on the top part of the lower window.

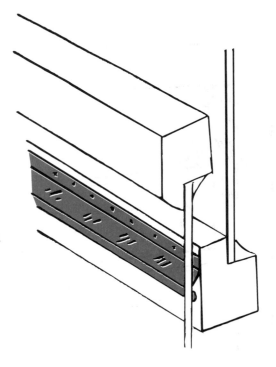

Step 3-5.
Installing rolled-vinyl gaskets.
With the window closed, fasten the strips on the outside of the window so that they can't be seen from the inside. Tack the vertical strips along the molding that forms the channels so that the rolled vinyl seals against the window.

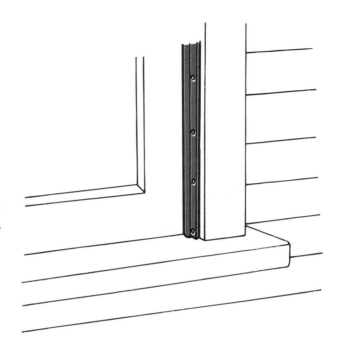

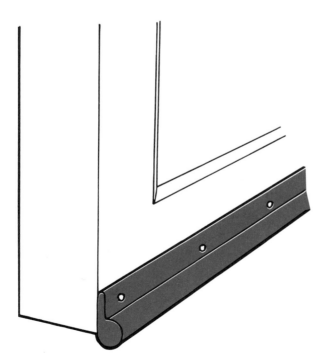

Step 3-6.
Installing the horizontal pieces.
Tack the horizontal pieces along the outside of the top of the upper window and the bottom of the lower window so that as the windows close, the rolled vinyl compresses slightly against the window opening.

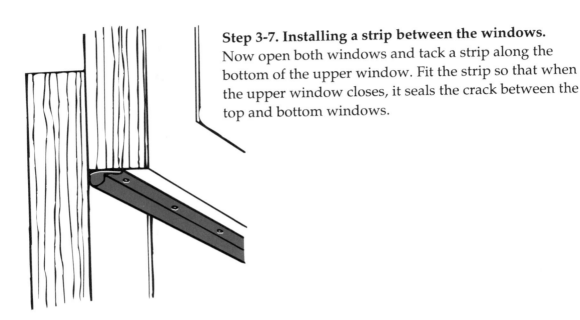

Step 3-7. Installing a strip between the windows.
Now open both windows and tack a strip along the bottom of the upper window. Fit the strip so that when the upper window closes, it seals the crack between the top and bottom windows.

**Step 3-8.
Installing adhesive-backed foam strips.**
This type of weatherstripping works best on casement windows; however, you can also use it on the top and bottom edges of double-hung or aluminum windows. Open the window and peel the protective tape from the foam. Fasten the foam against the window stop molding on the window opening. Place it so that when the window closes, it compresses the foam between the window and the window opening.

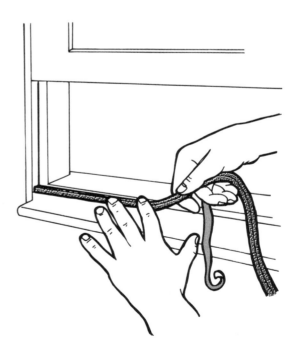

Step 3-9.
Installing plastic storm windows.
Measure the height of the largest
window to get the width of the roll
of plastic you need. Then measure
the width of all the windows to get
the sizes of the kits you need. If
you are buying the plastic in rolls,
add the widths of the windows
together to get the total running
feet. If you are going to attach the
plastic to the outside, you need to
cut it about 6 inches larger than the
window all around.

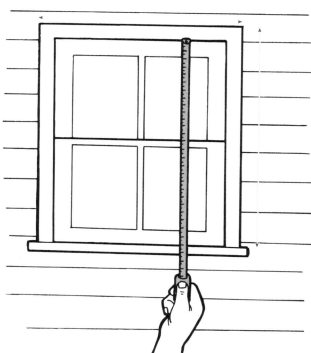

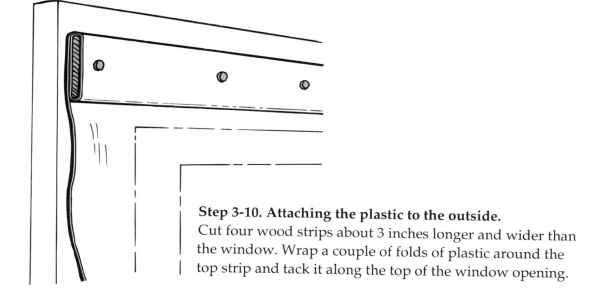

Step 3-10. Attaching the plastic to the outside.
Cut four wood strips about 3 inches longer and wider than
the window. Wrap a couple of folds of plastic around the
top strip and tack it along the top of the window opening.

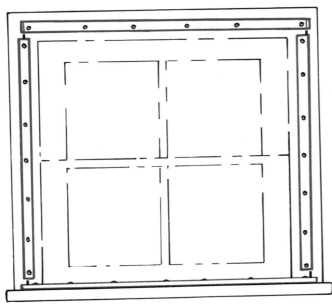

Step 3-11.
Attaching the bottom and sides.
Now wrap the bottom edge of the plastic a couple of turns around the bottom wood strip. Pull the plastic taut and tack the strip across the bottom of the window opening. Repeat the steps for fastening each side. If you attach the plastic to the inside of the window, stick it in place with masking tape.

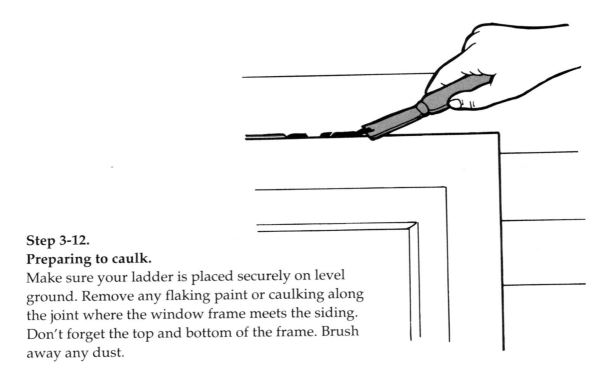

Step 3-12.
Preparing to caulk.
Make sure your ladder is placed securely on level ground. Remove any flaking paint or caulking along the joint where the window frame meets the siding. Don't forget the top and bottom of the frame. Brush away any dust.

Step 3-13. Caulking.

Run a smooth bead of caulking along the joint so that it adheres to both sides. Wipe off any excess with your fingertip or a dry cloth.

CHAPTER FOUR

Insulating Attics

Insulating an attic, or adding insulation, is not too difficult, just uncomfortable. If your attic has no insulation, lay insulation batts or blankets between the joists with the vapor-barrier side down toward the ceiling. If the attic is insulated, and the insulation comes up to the top of the joists, add an additional layer of unfaced batts (without a vapor barrier) across the joists. A typical unheated attic should have about a foot of fiberglass insulation in the floor. Remember, fiberglass insulation is extremely irritating to the skin. Wear loose clothing with long sleeves and tight-fitting openings, gloves, a dust mask, and goggles.

Tools & Materials

- ❏ Boards
- ❏ Drop lights
- ❏ Gloves
- ❏ Dust mask
- ❏ Goggles
- ❏ Insulation
- ❏ Utility knife
- ❏ Staple gun

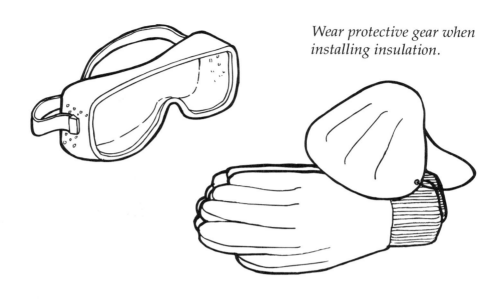

Wear protective gear when installing insulation.

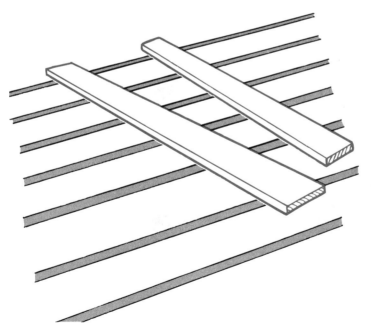

Step 4-1.
Preparing your work area.
Lay boards across the joists so you have something to kneel or stand on. A couple of 1×6s or a few pieces of 3/4-inch plywood should work. Hang a couple of drop lights from the rafters so you have plenty of light.

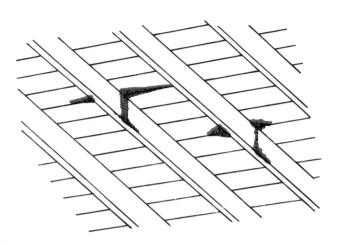

Step 4-2.
Checking for leaks.
Check the roof for any sign
of leaks and make the repairs
before installing the insulation.
You don't want any wet insulation.

Step 4-3.
Locating possible fire hazards.
Locate any recessed lights, vent fans, or other heat-producing devices.
You need to keep the insulation at least 3 inches from them due to the
fire hazard.

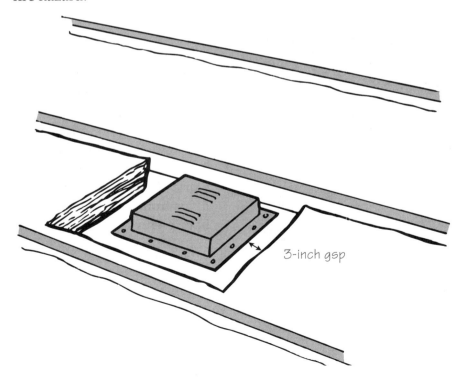

3-inch gap

Step 4-4.
Laying batts or blankets.
Insulation batts and blankets come in widths of 15 and 23 inches so that they fit snugly between either 16- or 24-inch centers of the joists. Lay the insulation between the joists with the vapor barrier down, working from the eaves toward the center so that you have more headroom for cutting and fitting.

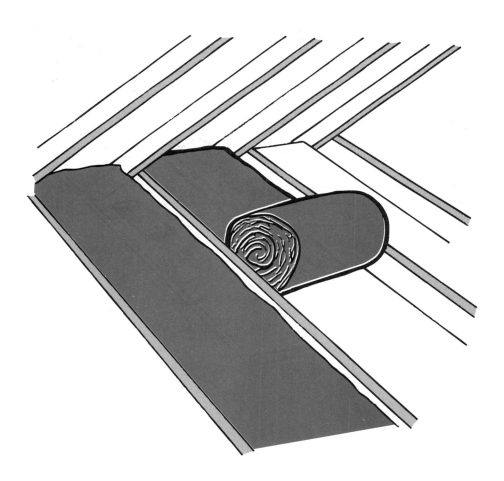

Step 4-5.
Positioning the insulation. Extend the insulation out far enough to cover the top plate in the wall but not far enough to cover the eaves vents into the attic.

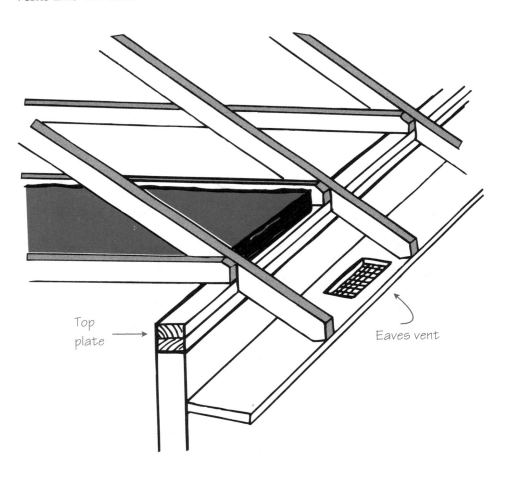

Top plate

Eaves vent

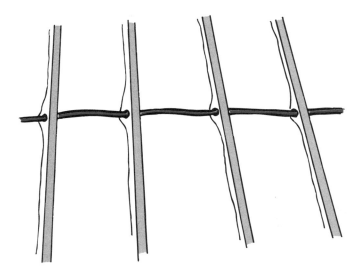

Step 4-6.
Insulating around wiring.
Slide the insulation under any wiring where possible. Be aware that sometimes, such as in older homes, placing insulation over electrical wiring might be a fire hazard. If in doubt, don't encase wiring in insulation, or check with your local building inspector.

Step 4-7.
Adding a second layer of insulation.
Lay rolls of the second layer across the joists, at right angles to the first layer. Work from the far ends toward the access hatch. The second layer should not have a vapor barrier.

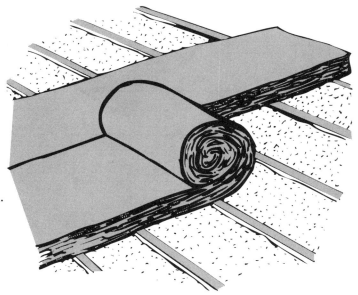

Step 4-8. Insulating the access hatch.

Staple a layer of insulation to the attic side of the hatch and check to be sure that the hatch fits tightly against the opening.

CHAPTER FIVE

Insulating Basements & Crawl Spaces

Insulating basements and crawl spaces can help cut down on heating costs. If your basement or crawl space is not heated, place the insulation between the joists under the ground-level floor. If the basement is heated, then insulate its perimeter walls. Keep in mind that any moisture in the basement defeats any method of insulation. If moisture is coming through the basement walls from the ground outside, you probably need to improve the drainage and provide a better seal against moisture from the outside.

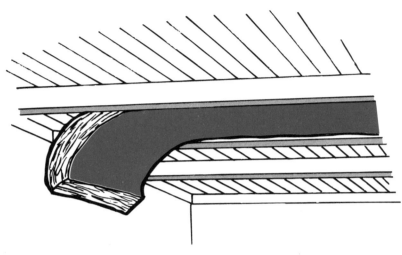

Insulate the ground-level floor in unheated crawl spaces or basements.

Insulate the outside walls in heated basements.

Tools & Materials

- ❏ Strips of insulation
- ❏ Caulking gun
- ❏ Caulking
- ❏ Foam gaskets for outlets
- ❏ Drop light
- ❏ Tape measure
- ❏ Chicken wire
- ❏ Heavy-duty staple gun and staples
- ❏ Gloves

- ❏ Goggles
- ❏ Dust mask
- ❏ Insulation batts or blankets with vapor barrier
- ❏ Utility knife
- ❏ Adhesive cartridges
- ❏ 4-x-8-foot foam insulation boards
- ❏ 4-x-8-foot sheets of gypsum board

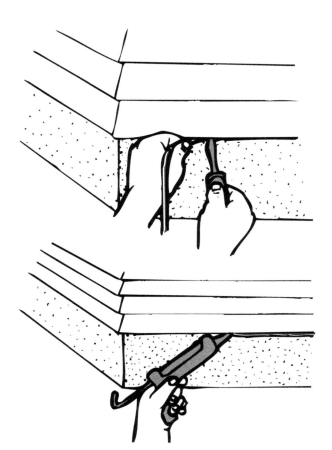

Step 5-1.
Stopping foundation drafts.
Air entering from the outside can often be felt around baseboards and electrical outlets. Fill larger cracks between the foundation and the outside walls with strips of insulation; then apply a layer of caulking. *Note:* The bottom edge of stucco walls might have openings to allow water to drain out. Don't seal those openings.

Step 5-2. Stopping drafts from electrical outlets.

Install precut foam gaskets behind the outlet covers. Simply remove the cover, fit the gasket in place, and then replace the cover.

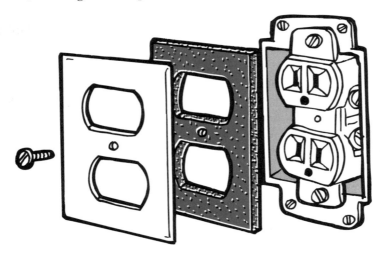

Step 5-3. Insulating an unheated crawl space.

Start at a perimeter wall and work out. Working in sections, staple chicken wire at right angles across the bottom of the joists.

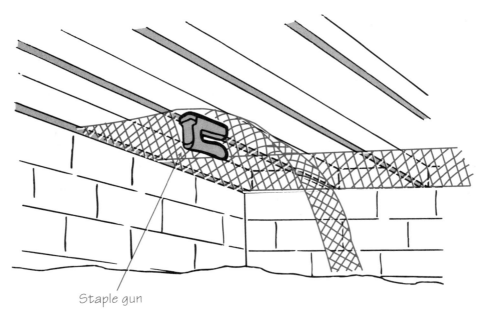

Staple gun

Step 5-4. Placing the insulation.

Hold the first batt with the vapor barrier up and fold the end up about 10 inches (the height of the board at the end of the joists) . Slide the batt between the joists on top of the chicken wire. Place the insulation with the vapor barrier facing up toward the heated rooms. Make sure the end of the batt that is folded up fits snugly against the underside of the floor at the end of the joist.

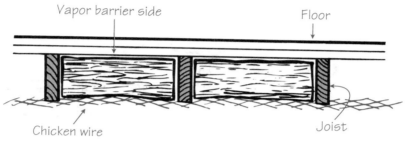

To insulate a heated basement, you can frame out the walls with 2×4s and install the insulation between the studs, or you can glue 4-×-8-foot foam insulation boards to the basement walls and cover them with gypsum board. The easier way uses the foam boards.

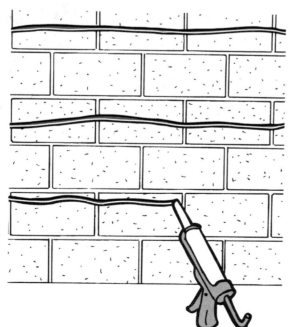

Step 5-5.
Applying the adhesive.
Use the caulking gun to apply the adhesive in parallel horizontal beads about a foot apart across the basement wall.

Step 5-6. Installing and covering the foam boards.

Press the foam boards firmly against the walls. Allow the glue to set for a few days, then cover all the insulation with 1/2-inch gypsum board for a fire barrier.

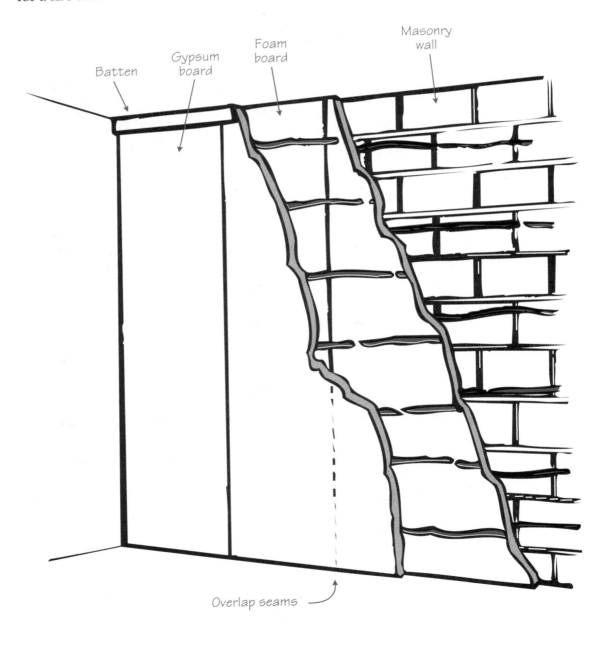

Batten

Gypsum board

Foam board

Masonry wall

Overlap seams

Step 5-7. Completing the job.

Next, cut batts to fit the header (the board at the end of the
overhead joists) and staple them in place with the vapor
barrier facing in towards you.

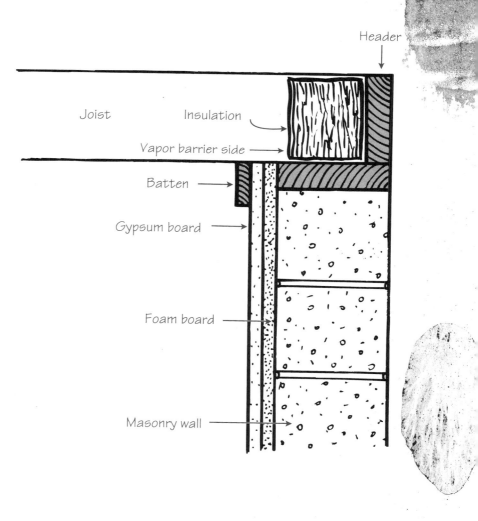

Header

Joist

Insulation

Vapor barrier side

Batten

Gypsum board

Foam board

Masonry wall

CHAPTER SIX

Insulating Water Heaters & Pipes

About 20 percent of the energy used in the home goes to heat water. If your water heater feels warm to the touch, it probably needs to be insulated. Fiberglass blankets for water heaters are available in kits at most hardware and building supply stores, or you can use leftover insulation. Just remember not to cover the top of a gas water heater or you'll block the air to the flue. Also, be careful not to block the airflow to the gas burner at the bottom of the heater.

Tools & Materials

- ❏ Gloves
- ❏ Goggles
- ❏ Dust mask
- ❏ Utility knife
- ❏ Fiberglass insulation (kit or blanket)
- ❏ Molded pipe insulation
- ❏ Duct tape

Step 6-1. Installing the insulation.

Cut the fiberglass blanket to fit around the tank and fasten the joint with duct tape. If the blanket has paper or foil backing, place the backing facing out.

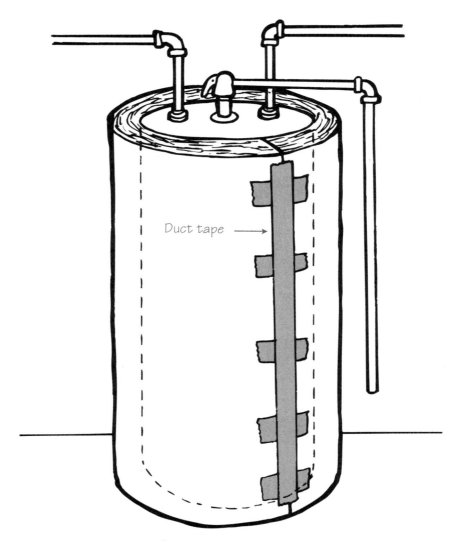

Duct tape

Step 6-2. Insulating electric water heaters.

If the water heater is electric, fit the insulation down to the floor and cover the top of the heater. Make sure to seal the top and the sides with tape. Cut out access openings for the upper and lower heating elements and thermostat. Be sure to leave the pressure relief valve and pipe exposed, and don't obstruct the discharge pipe or the drain valve.

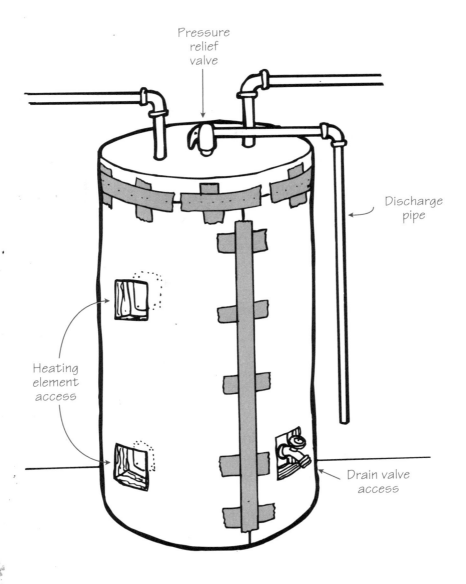

Pressure relief valve

Discharge pipe

Heating element access

Drain valve access

Step 6-3. Insulating gas water heaters.

If the heater is gas, do not cover the top of the heater and do not put any insulation near the burner. All flammable material should be kept well clear of the flue pipe. Otherwise, you'll create a fire hazard; you also could void your homeowner's insurance.

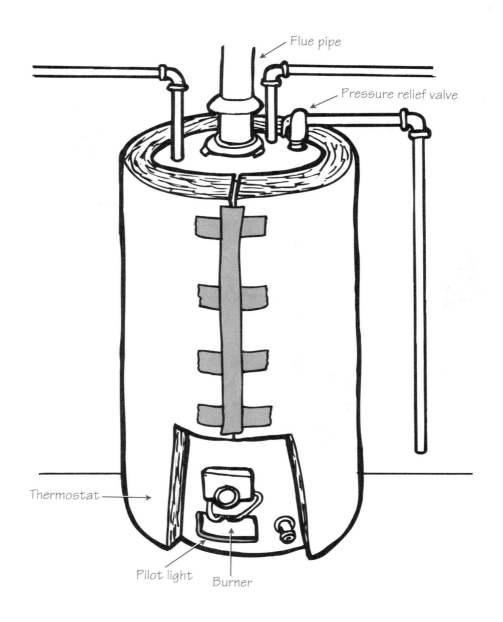

Flue pipe

Pressure relief valve

Thermostat

Pilot light   Burner

Step 6-4. Insulating hot-water pipes.

Install preslit foam sleeves over the pipes and give the sleeves a twist to hold them in place. You also can use foam tape with an adhesive backing. Simply peel off the protective strip and wrap the tape around the pipe.

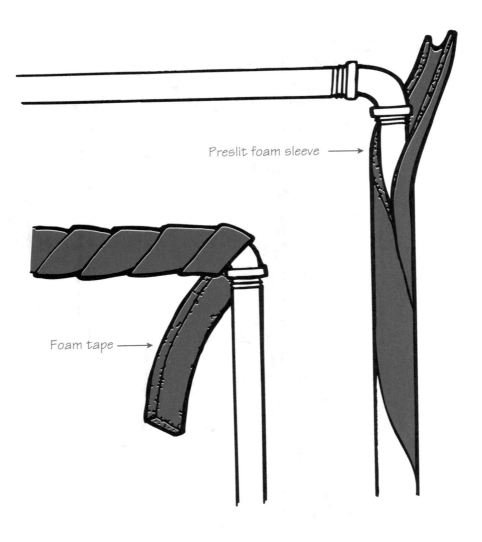

Preslit foam sleeve

Foam tape

CHAPTER SEVEN

Stopping Faucet Leaks

Next to the air we breathe, water is probably the most precious resource in our lives. It is in limited supply. The total amount of water on the earth always remains the same. It only changes its form and moves in cycles from the oceans to the land and then back to the oceans. A typical home uses thousands of gallons of water every year, but a lot goes down the drain needlessly. A slow drip from a leaky faucet wastes 15 to 20 gallons a day.

Faucets can be divided into two basic types: stem faucets and single-lever faucets. You usually can repair a leaky stem faucet by replacing a washer. Repair kits are available at most hardware stores for single-lever ball or cartridge faucets. The steps in this chapter can help hold down water bills and conserve this essential commodity.

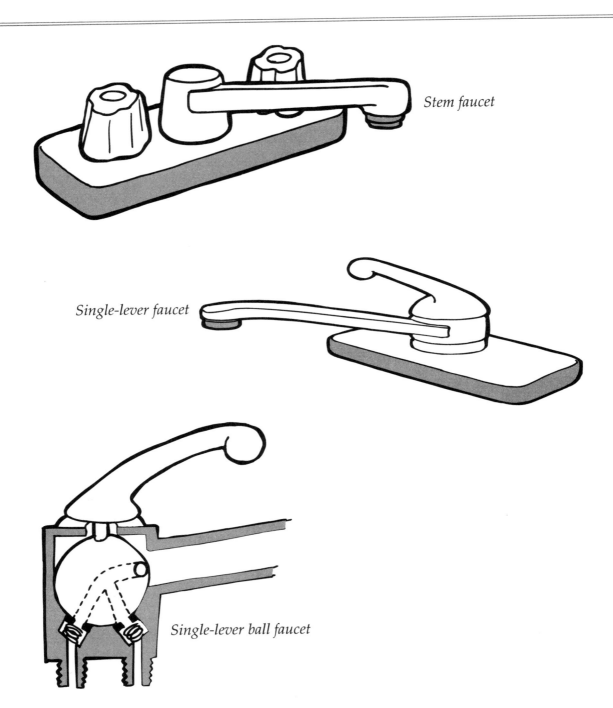

Stem faucet

Single-lever faucet

Single-lever ball faucet

Single-lever cartridge faucet

Ceramic-disc cartridge

Tools & Materials

- Small screwdriver
- Adjustable wrench
- Rag or paper towel
- Flashlight
- Hex wrench
- Faucet seat wrench
- Penetrating oil
- Faucet seat dresser
- Petroleum jelly
- Knife
- Needle-nose pliers
- Pliers
- Plumber's socket wrench
- Washers, O-rings, or repair kit

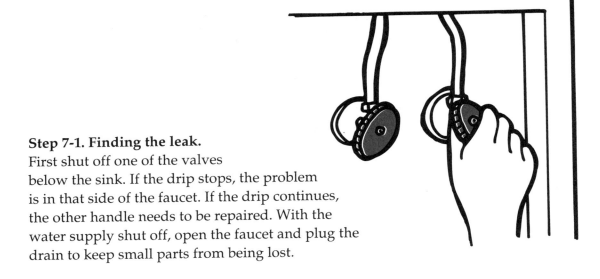

Step 7-1. Finding the leak.
First shut off one of the valves
below the sink. If the drip stops, the problem
is in that side of the faucet. If the drip continues,
the other handle needs to be repaired. With the
water supply shut off, open the faucet and plug the
drain to keep small parts from being lost.

Step 7-2. Getting to the stem.
Pry off the trim cap with the tip of a knife or
small screwdriver. Now remove the screw holding
the handle and lift off the handle. The stem is held
in place with a locknut or a packing nut. If it is a
packing nut, protect the finish with tape. Use an
adjustable wrench to remove the packing nut
or locknut.

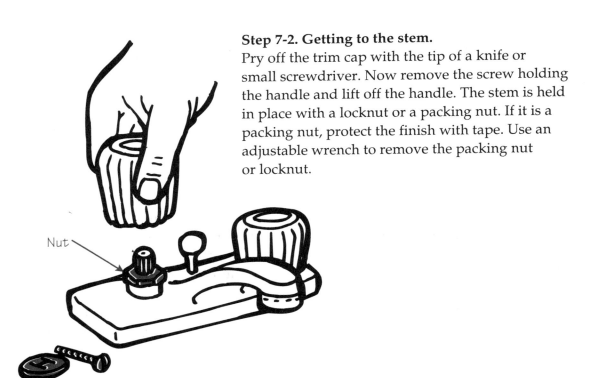

Nut

Step 7-3.
Removing the stem.
If the stem had a packing nut, the stem is threaded into the faucet. Place the handle back on the stem and turn it counterclockwise to remove it. If the stem had a locknut, wiggle the stem slightly and lift it from the faucet body.

Step 7-4.

Replacing the washer on a standard stem.
Remove the screw in the bottom of the stem and pry out the old washer with the tip of a knife or small screwdriver. Install the new washer. If the washer is tapered, the tapered end should face down toward the faucet seat. Make sure the top of the washer fits snugly into the stem cup. Install a new screw and tighten it until it begins to compress the washer slightly.

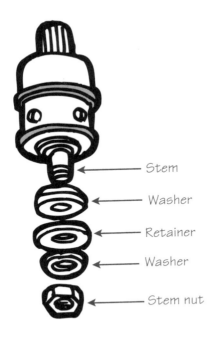

Stem

Washer

Retainer

Washer

Stem nut

Step 7-5.
Replacing a washer on reverse-pressure stem.
Use an adjustable wrench to remove the nut on the bottom of the stem. Remove the nut washer, washer retainer, and the stem washer. Install the new stem washer with the tapered side up toward the faucet seat. Next, install the washer retainer, nut washer, and nut.

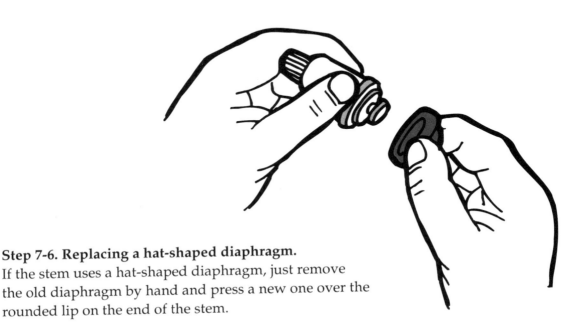

Step 7-6. Replacing a hat-shaped diaphragm.
If the stem uses a hat-shaped diaphragm, just remove the old diaphragm by hand and press a new one over the rounded lip on the end of the stem.

Step 7-7.
Checking the faucet seat.
If the faucet continues to drip after you replace the washer, the problem is probably with the faucet seat. Remove the stem assembly and examine the faucet seat. You might have to soak up water over the seat with a small piece of rag or paper towel. Run your finger over the seat's surface. Use a flashlight to check for pits or cuts.

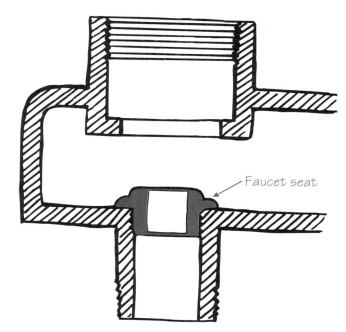

Faucet seat

Step 7-8.
Replacing the faucet seat.
If you found any pits or cuts in the faucet seat, remove the seat with a hex wrench or the hexagonal end of a faucet seat wrench. Turn the old seat counterclockwise to remove it. If the seat is frozen, apply a little penetrating oil and wait a few minutes. Start the new seat by hand and tighten it with the seat wrench. In some faucets, the seat is part of the faucet body and cannot be removed. You can grind these seats smooth with a faucet seat dresser.

Step 7-9. Dressing the seat.

Faucet seat dressers come with several sizes of cutters and seat guides, and they can be expensive. You might try renting instead of buying. Select the largest cutter that fits the faucet seat and a guide that fits the seat hole. With the cutter and guide installed on the tool, screw the guide cone down snugly into the faucet body. Now turn the knob on the tool a few smooth, steady turns. Don't press down on the tool too much. The seat is made of soft brass and cuts easily. After a few turns, the knob will be easy to turn. The seat should now be dressed. Remove the tool and wipe away the filings with a damp rag. Reassemble the faucet and check it for leaks. If it still leaks, repeat the seat-dressing process. If dressing the seat fails to stop the leak, you might have to replace the faucet.

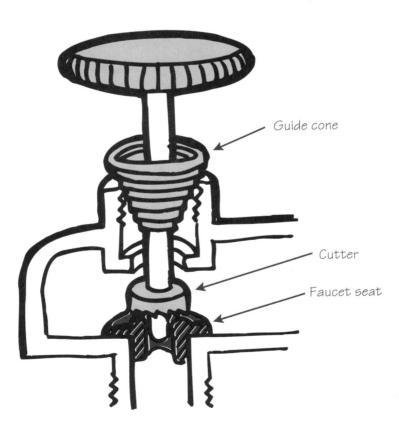

Guide cone

Cutter

Faucet seat

Sometimes water seeps up near the handle of the faucet and leaks from around the top of the faucet stem. The way you stop this kind of leak depends on the type of faucet. If the faucet has a packing nut, you probably need to replace the packing washer or packing material. If the faucet has a locknut, the O-ring is probably bad.

Step 7-10. Stem leaking on a faucet with a packing nut.
First, try gently tightening the packing nut. If the leak doesn't stop, shut off the water supply valve beneath the sink, and remove the faucet handle. Remove the packing nut and replace the packing washer. If the stem has packing material, add a few turns of new packing string or pipe tape to the old packing. Screw the packing nut back on. The packing nut should compress the packing, but don't overtighten it. Reinstall the handle and turn the water supply back on.

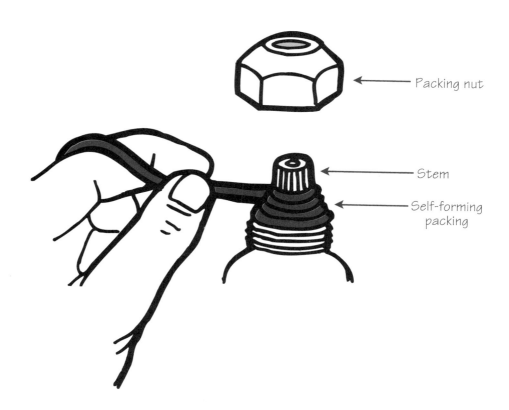

Packing nut

Stem

Self-forming packing

Step 7-11. Stem leaking on a faucet with a locknut.
This faucet stem should have an O-ring. Shut off the water supply
valve beneath the sink and remove the stem assembly. Press the
O-ring from the sides so that part of it comes out of the O-ring groove,
and then roll the O-ring off the stem. Take it with you to buy a new
one. You need an exact replacement. Discard the old one so you don't
accidentally reinstall it. Lubricate the new O-ring with petroleum jelly,
slip it on the stem, and reassemble the faucet.

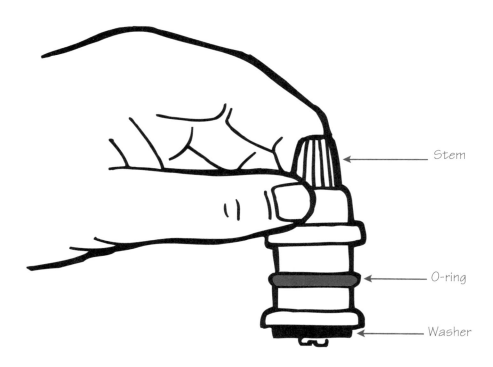

Single-lever faucets come in variations of three basic models: ball faucets, sleeve-cartridge faucets, and ceramic-disc cartridge faucets. You can make repairs easily with prepackaged repair kits or by installing a new cartridge.

Step 7-12. Tightening the adjusting ring on a ball faucet.
You can often fix a dripping ball faucet by just tightening the adjusting ring. Use a hex wrench to loosen the setscrew at the base of the handle and remove the handle. With the handle removed, you should see a ring with notches at the top of a protective cap. Place the edge of a dinner knife across the notches in the ring and turn the ring clockwise. Don't overtighten it. You should be able to move the ball with the handle removed. If tightening the adjusting ring fails to stop the leak, you'll have to take the faucet apart.

Step 7-13. Disassembling the ball faucet.

First turn off both water supply valves beneath the sink, and then open the faucet. Remove the handle. Unscrew the protective cap and remove the cap and adjusting ring. Lift out the plastic cam, cam washer, and rotating ball. Gently wiggle the spout and lift it up from the spout collar. You should now have access to the rubber faucet seats, springs, and the spout O-rings.

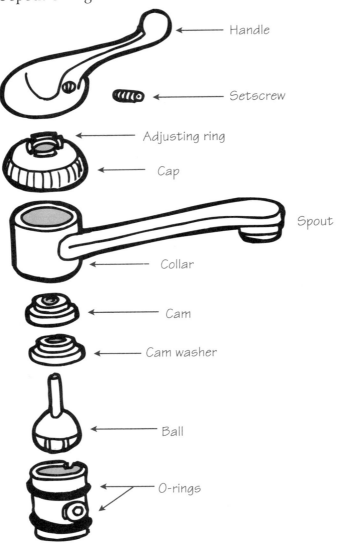

Step 7-14.
Replacing seats and O-rings in a ball faucet.
The rubber seats are held against the bottom of
the ball by small springs. Use the point of a
screwdriver to remove the two seats and springs.
Note how the rubber seats fit against the springs.
The new ones must be installed the same way.
Install new seats and springs from a repair
kit, and replace the O-ring on the spout
collar. Lower the spout straight down
over the collar to prevent damage to
the O-rings. Reassemble the faucet
and turn on the water supply.

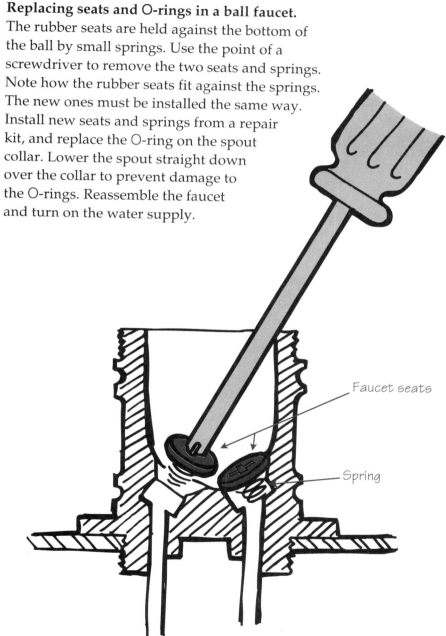

Faucet seats

Spring

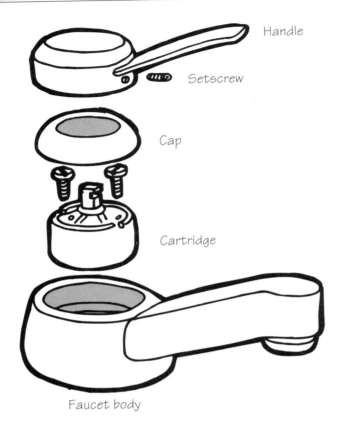

Handle

Setscrew

Cap

Cartridge

Faucet body

Step 7-15.
Repairing a faucet with a ceramic-disc cartridge.

First, turn off both water supply valves beneath the sink, and then open the faucet. Use a hex wrench to loosen the setscrew at the base of the handle. Some setscrews are hidden behind a decorative button. Pry the button off with a small screwdriver. With the setscrew loosened, remove the handle. Beneath the handle is a cap that might be screwed on or held on by a plastic adapter. Unscrew the cap or pry it off.

Step 7-16.
Checking the cartridge.

Remove the two or three screws holding the cartridge in place and lift out the cartridge. Check the cartridge for cracks or pits, and replace it if necessary. Install new seals and align the cartridge in the faucet body so that the three holes line up. Install the cartridge screws, but don't overtighten. Reassemble the faucet.

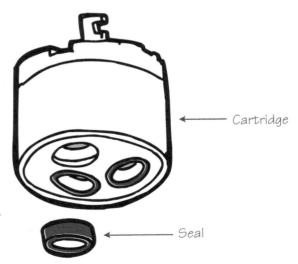

Cartridge

Seal

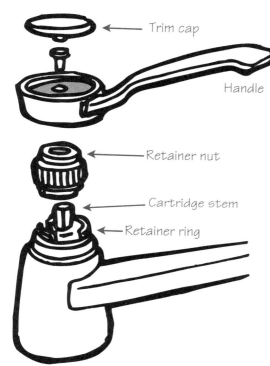

Trim cap

Handle

Retainer nut

Cartridge stem

Retainer ring

Step 7-17.
Servicing a sleeve-cartridge faucet.
To service a sleeve-cartridge faucet, first shut off both water supply valves beneath the sink, and then open the faucet. Pry off the trim cover with the tip of a knife or a small screwdriver. Remove the screw that holds the handle and tilt the handle up to release it from the retainer nut. Use an adjustable wrench to remove the retainer nut.

Step 7-18. Removing the clip.
Find the U-shaped clip that holds in the cartridge. Use the tip of a screwdriver or needle-nose pliers to pull out the clip.

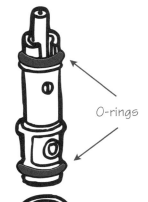

O-rings

Step 7-19. Replacing the cartridge O-rings.
Use pliers to lift out the cartridge. It fits tightly in the faucet body. Replace any damaged O-rings and lubricate the new ones with petroleum jelly. If the cartridge is worn, replace it. Install the new cartridge, making sure it is properly aligned, and reassemble the faucet.

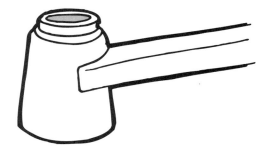

Step 7-20. Replacing spout O-rings.
To replace the spout O-rings, remove the retainer nut and lift off the spout. Replace the O-rings, lubricating the new ones with petroleum jelly.

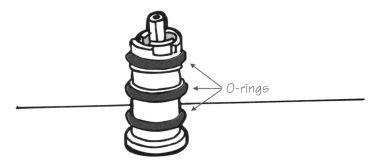

O-rings

Repairing tub and shower faucets is just like fixing sink faucets. The problem is getting to the stem. First, you'll need a deep socket and ratchet—or a plumber's socket wrench of the appropriate size—to remove the bonnet. The bonnet is the housing that contains most of the stem.

Step 7-21. Getting to the bonnet.

First turn off the water supply and open the faucet. If shutoff valves are not available, shut off the main water supply valve into the house. Then pry off the handle cover with the tip of a knife or small screwdriver. Now remove the screw, handle, and sleeve. You should see the bonnet nut. It might be covered with joint cement or plaster. If so, carefully chip the material away to allow room for the socket wrench.

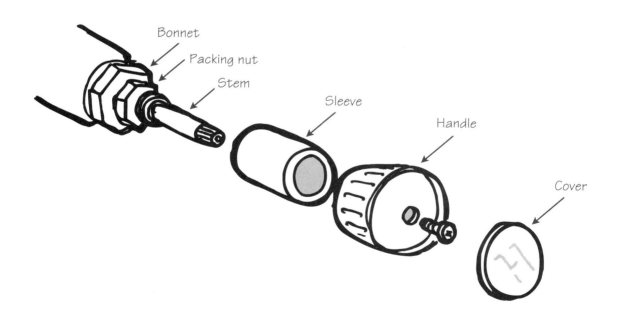

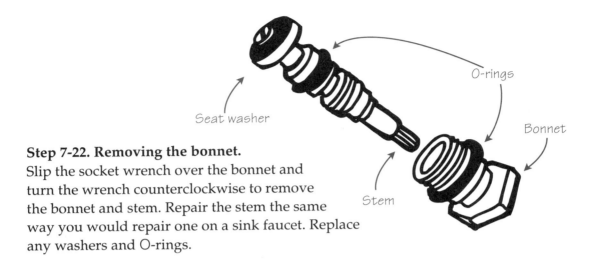

Seat washer

O-rings

Bonnet

Stem

Step 7-22. Removing the bonnet.

Slip the socket wrench over the bonnet and turn the wrench counterclockwise to remove the bonnet and stem. Repair the stem the same way you would repair one on a sink faucet. Replace any washers and O-rings.

Step 7-23. Dressing the faucet seat.

If necessary, dress or replace the faucet seat. You can repair ball faucets and cartridge faucets the same way you fix the corresponding type of sink faucet.

Faucet seat dresser or seat dressing tool

Faucet seat

CHAPTER EIGHT

Stopping Toilet Leaks

Toilets operate on a simple principle: A lever trips a flush valve, which releases a volume of water from a tank. The water swirls into a bowl, then travels through a water-filled trap into a waste line. As the water leaves the tank, a float drops down and opens another valve, called a ball cock, causing a smaller flow of water to refill the tank. At the same time, gravity closes the flush valve. When the water reaches a certain level, the float closes the ball cock, shutting off the water to the tank, and the system is ready to use again.

The tank and bowl are made of porcelain and will last almost forever. However, the parts inside the tank that operate the system are made of brass or plastic, and will eventually corrode or wear out and need to be replaced. The most common problem is water running continuously after the toilet is flushed. Occasionally, leaks from the tank do occur. To check for a leaky toilet, drop a little food coloring in the tank in the evening. If the water in the bowl is a different color in the morning, the flush valve is leaking. Flush valves are easily replaced.

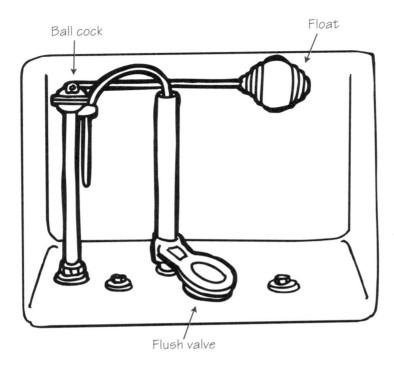

Ball cock

Float

Flush valve

Inside a typical tank.

Tools & Materials

- ❏ Food coloring
- ❏ Pliers
- ❏ Fine steel wool
- ❏ Small screwdriver
- ❏ Knife
- ❏ Old toothbrush
- ❏ Vinegar
- ❏ Sponge or rag
- ❏ Adjustable wrench
- ❏ Locking pliers
- ❏ Flush valve, ball cock, or repair kit

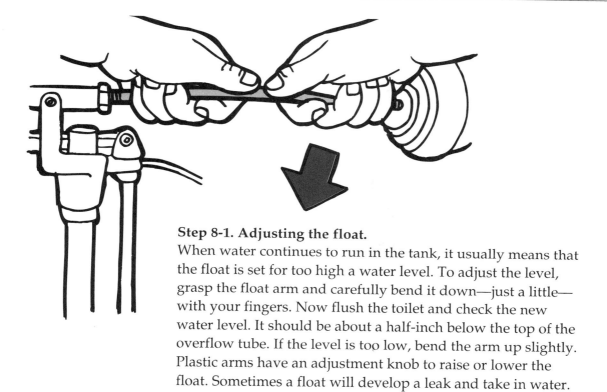

Step 8-1. Adjusting the float.

When water continues to run in the tank, it usually means that the float is set for too high a water level. To adjust the level, grasp the float arm and carefully bend it down—just a little—with your fingers. Now flush the toilet and check the new water level. It should be about a half-inch below the top of the overflow tube. If the level is too low, bend the arm up slightly. Plastic arms have an adjustment knob to raise or lower the float. Sometimes a float will develop a leak and take in water.

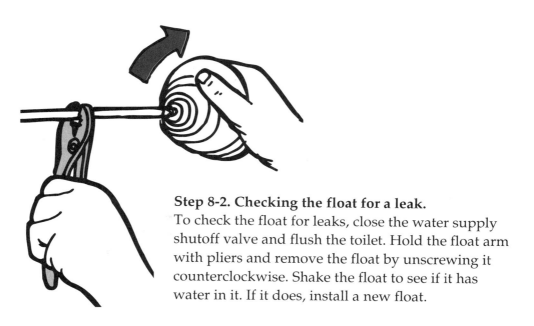

Step 8-2. Checking the float for a leak.

To check the float for leaks, close the water supply shutoff valve and flush the toilet. Hold the float arm with pliers and remove the float by unscrewing it counterclockwise. Shake the float to see if it has water in it. If it does, install a new float.

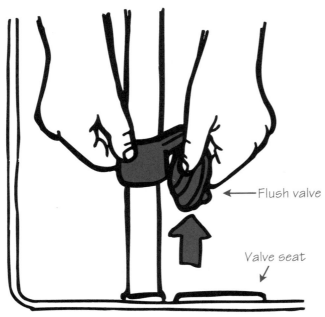

Flush valve

Valve seat

Step 8-3.
Stopping a flush valve leak.
When water runs continuously from the tank into the bowl, the flush valve is probably not sealing properly. It might be a flapper or ball flush valve. To clean the valve seat, first turn off the water supply valve and flush the toilet to empty the tank. Unhook the flush valve—or loosen the clamp screw—and slide the valve up the overflow tube.

Step 8-4. Cleaning the valve seat.
Use fine steel wool and gently scrub any mineral deposits or sediment from the valve seat. Wash the sediment into the bowl and reinstall the valve. Turn on the water supply and check for leaks. If the flapper or ball is badly worn or distorted, install a new one.

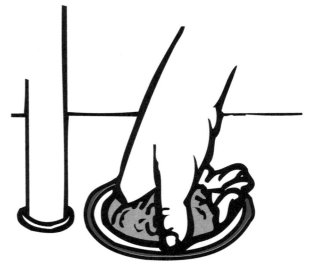

Step 8-5.
Removing a ball cock with a plunger.
To repair the ball cock, first shut off the water supply and flush the toilet. For a ball cock with a plunger, remove the two thumbscrews and slide out the float arm. Now lift out the plunger.

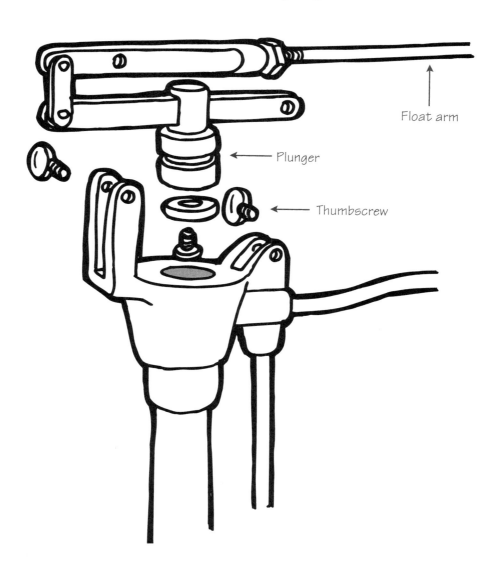

Float arm

Plunger

Thumbscrew

Step 8-6. Removing a ball cock with a diaphragm.

On a ball cock with a diaphragm, remove the screws holding the bonnet in place and lift off the float arm and bonnet. You should now have access to the washers on the plunger or diaphragm in the bonnet.

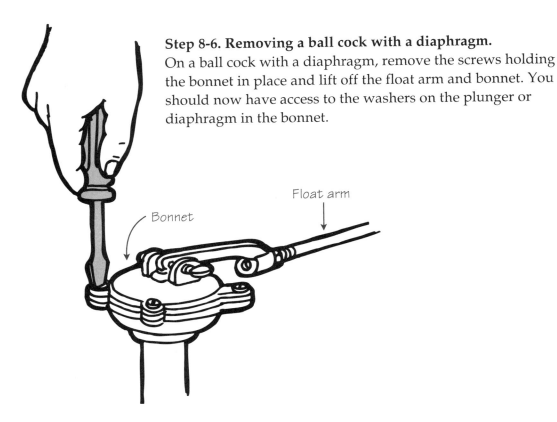

Step 8-7. Cleaning the parts.

Use the tip of a knife or small screwdriver to remove the washers or diaphragm. Use an old toothbrush and vinegar to scrub away any sediment and install new washers or a new diaphragm. Reassemble the ball cock and turn on the water supply. Flush the toilet and test for leaks. If the toilet still runs continuously, install a new ball cock.

Step 8-8. Replacing the ball cock.

To replace the ball cock, first shut off the water and flush the toilet. Drain as much water from the tank as you can and sponge up any excess. Unscrew the float arm and float from the ball cock. Now you need to disconnect the water supply tube underneath the tank. Use an adjustable wrench to disconnect the water supply tube from the tank. You might need to disconnect the tube from the shutoff valve and remove it completely.

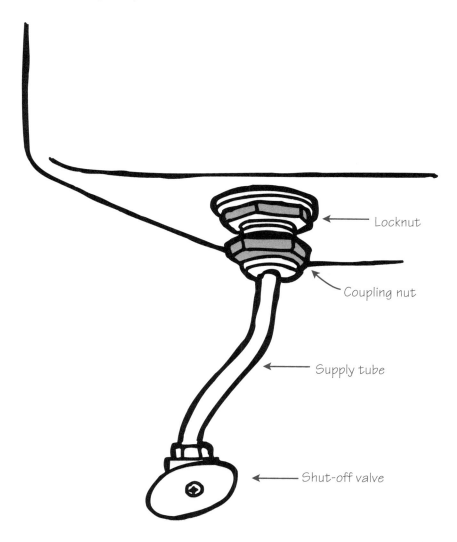

Locknut

Coupling nut

Supply tube

Shut-off valve

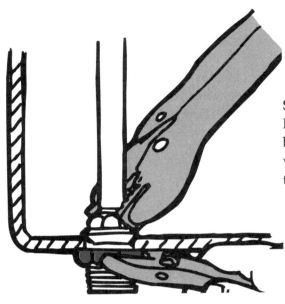

Step 8-9. Removing the old ball cock.
Inside the tank, grip the ball cock at its
base with locking pliers. Use an adjustable
wrench to unscrew the locknut under the
tank. Now lift the ball cock from the tank.

Step 8-10.
Installing the new ball cock.
Install the cone-shaped washer on the
threaded base of the new ball cock
and then insert the ball cock into the
opening in the tank. Hold the ball
cock in position with one hand while
you thread the locknut on with the
other. Tighten the locknut as tight as
you can by hand, then turn it about a
half turn with an adjustable wrench.
Reinstall the float arm and float.
Reconnect the water supply tube and
turn on the water. You'll probably
have to adjust the float for the correct
water level.

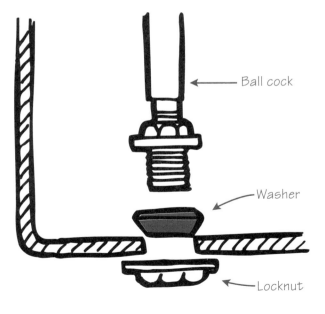

CHAPTER NINE

Installing Energy-efficient Lighting

About 10 percent of the energy used in the home goes for lighting. It doesn't cost much, maybe $100 a year, but it's enough that doing something about reducing those costs is worthwhile, since energy-efficient alternatives are available. Most home lighting is provided by incandescent lights—the regular light bulbs commonly found in home fixtures and lamps. With these types of light bulbs, only about 10 percent of the electricity used produces the light, while the rest ends up as heat. Your air conditioner works harder in the summer, and you're paying for an expensive form of heat in the winter.

Living and dining areas often have overhead lights that are too bright for all situations. Dimmer switches allow you to vary the intensity to suit the mood, reducing electrical consumption when the dimmer is turned to any point below full bright. Most dimmer switches, however, can be used only with incandescent lights.

You can replace regular lamp sockets with three-way sockets, and screw bulbs or adapters into lamp sockets to allow you to use fluorescent tubes. Fluorescent lights use about one-fourth as much electricity as incandescent lights and last nearly ten times longer. Often, compact fluorescent lights are too tall or wide to fit existing fixtures. Standard lamps might require a larger bracket to hold the shade. Some fluorescent adapters have slots to hold the bracket, but the shade probably will be raised a little. Some trial and error might be necessary to find just what you want. Just remember—don't use fluorescent lights where you have a dimmer switch.

In this chapter and chapter 11, you need to perform tests with a volt-ohmmeter or neon voltage tester. Familiarize yourself with the owner's manual that comes with the meter. The main points to remember: When making voltage tests, always keep your fingers on the insulated part of the probes; and be sure the meter is set on the proper voltage scale, not on the resistance scale. Follow proper safety precautions whenever you are working around electricity.

Tools and Materials

❏ Screwdriver
❏ Neon voltage tester
　 or volt-ohmmeter
❏ Wire nuts
❏ Needle-nose pliers
❏ Wire
❏ Wire stripper
❏ Dimmer switch

❏ Three-way socket
❏ Fluorescent light fixture
❏ Fixture bar and stud
❏ Large metal washer
❏ Fixture jumper wires
　 (black, white, and green)
❏ Toggle bolts or other fasteners

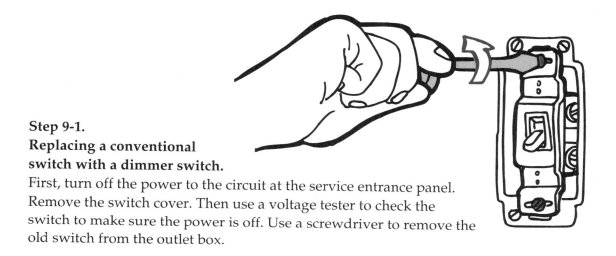

Step 9-1.
Replacing a conventional switch with a dimmer switch.

First, turn off the power to the circuit at the service entrance panel. Remove the switch cover. Then use a voltage tester to check the switch to make sure the power is off. Use a screwdriver to remove the old switch from the outlet box.

Step 9-2. Disconnecting the wires.

Disconnect the two wires going to the switch. Use a screwdriver if the wires are attached to screw terminals. If the switch is back-wired, insert a small screwdriver into the slots next to the wires to release the wires.

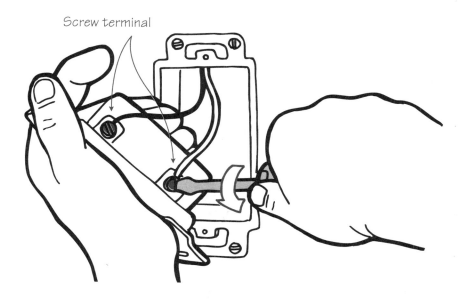

Screw terminal

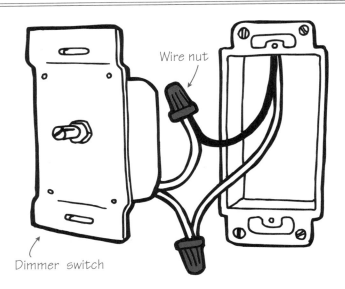

Step 9-3.
Connecting the wires.
The dimmer switch has two wires. Use wire nuts to connect each house wire to each of the two wires on the dimmer switch. Either switch wire can be connected to either house wire. Place the bare ends of the wires together and screw on a wire nut.

Wire nut

Dimmer switch

Step 9-4. Mounting the switch.
Carefully fold the wires into the box and mount the switch the same way the old switch was mounted. Install the cover plate and press the knob on the switch, completing the job.

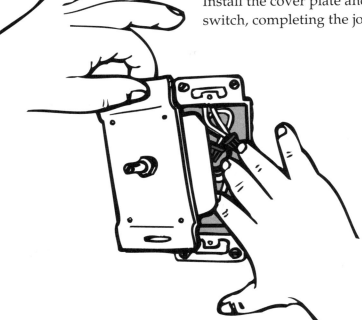

Step 9-5.
Replacing a lamp socket with a three-way socket.
First unplug the lamp. Then remove the shade, shade bracket, and bulb. Examine the outer shell of the socket for a place marked PRESS. It should be near the switch. Hold the cap (the bottom of the socket) steady with one hand while pressing the mark on the shell.

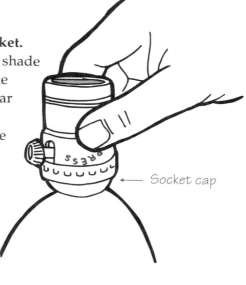

← Socket cap

Step 9-6. Removing the shell.
Twist the shell slightly and remove it from the cap.

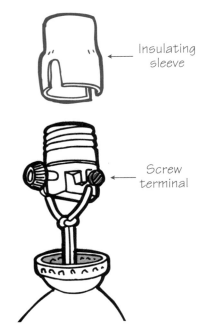

Insulating sleeve

Screw terminal

Step 9-7.
Inside the lamp socket.
Beneath the outer shell, you should find an insulating sleeve covering the socket. Remove the insulating sleeve and you'll see the screw terminals.

Step 9-8. Removing the socket.
Use a screwdriver to disconnect the two wires going to the terminal screws, and remove the socket, leaving the socket cap in place. The new socket will come with a socket cap, but usually you don't need to replace the old one. Reconnect the wires to the two screw terminals on the three-way socket, and install the new socket.

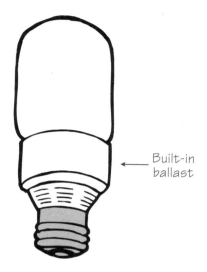

Built-in
ballast

Step 9-9.
Using integral compact fluorescent lights.
All fluorescent lights need a ballast to operate.
Integral compact fluorescent lights have the
ballast built into the base of the bulb. Just screw
the light into a conventional socket.

Step 9-10.
Using modular compact fluorescent lights.
Modular compact fluorescent lights have a separate
ballast and tube. In this case, you don't have to
replace the ballast when the tube burns out. Screw
the ballast into a conventional socket and plug the tube
into the ballast.

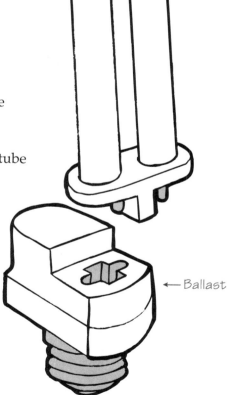

Ballast

Step 9-11.

Replacing an incandescent fixture with a fluorescent fixture.

First, turn off the power to the circuit at the service entrance panel. Remove the globe if the fixture has one. Then remove the light bulbs. Now disconnect the fixture from the wall or ceiling, and disconnect the fixture wires from the house wires. The old fixture should now be free from the outlet box.

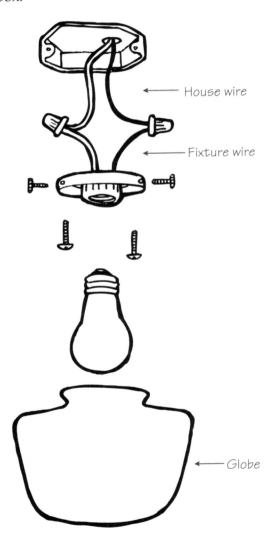

House wire

Fixture wire

Globe

Step 9-12. Installing jumper wires.

Cut two pieces of the jumper wire (the same kind used with the fixture) about 8 inches long. One should be black, the other white. Now cut two more 8-inch wires for the ground wire. This wire should be bare copper or green insulated wire. With the wire stripper, remove about a half-inch of the insulation from each end of the insulated wires.

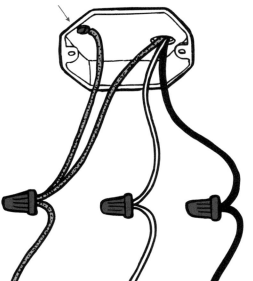

Grounding
screw

Step 9-13. Connecting the jumper wires.

Use wire nuts to connect the black jumper wire to the black house wire, and the white jumper wire to the white house wire. Use a wire nut to connect the two ground wires to the ground house wire. Now connect the other end of one ground jumper wire to the grounding screw in the outlet box. Grounding screws are often green, but any screw that clamps the wire to bare metal will work. You now should have the free ends of one black, one white, and one ground wire coming from the outlet box.

Step 9-14. Installing the fixture bar and stud.

Thread the stud into the fixture bar, and run the wires through the hole in the stud. Now fold the house wires into the box, leaving the jumper wires extending down through the stud. Use screws to fasten each end of the bar to the box.

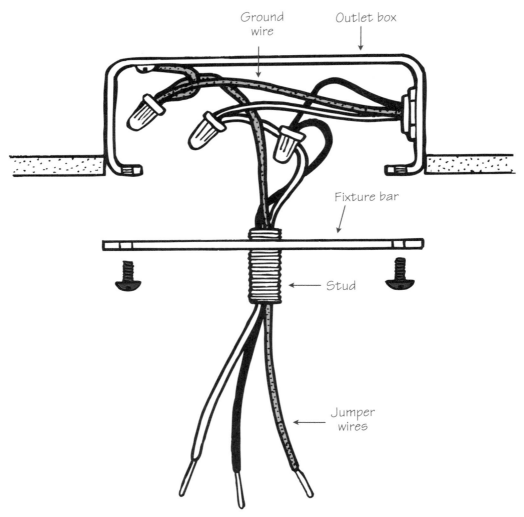

Step 9-15. Attaching the fixture.

Remove the fluorescent fixture's plastic tube covering and any tubes. Remove a knockout from the back of the fixture and slide the fixture over the wires and stud attached to the box. Place the large metal washer over the stud for extra support and screw the locknut onto the stud. Tighten the locknut with an adjustable wrench.

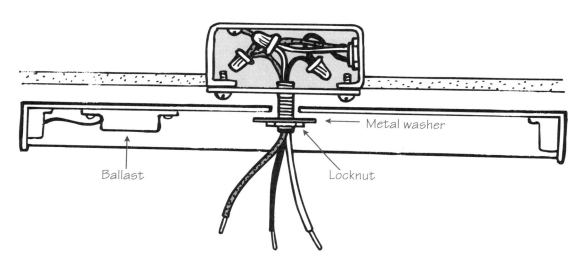

Metal washer

Ballast

Locknut

Step 9-16. Connecting the wires.

Use wire nuts to connect the black fixture wire to the black jumper wire, and the white fixture wire to the white jumper wire. Now connect the ground wire to the grounding screw in the base of the fixture.

Grounding screw

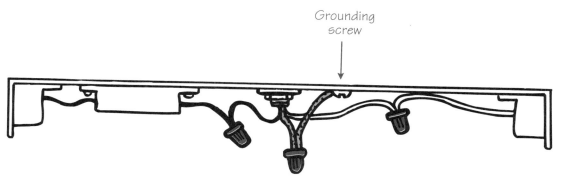

Step 9-17. Providing additional support for larger fixtures.
If your fixture needs additional support, drill a hole at each end of the
base of the fixture and install screws. If the mounting surface is
wallboard, use appropriate fasteners such as toggle bolts.

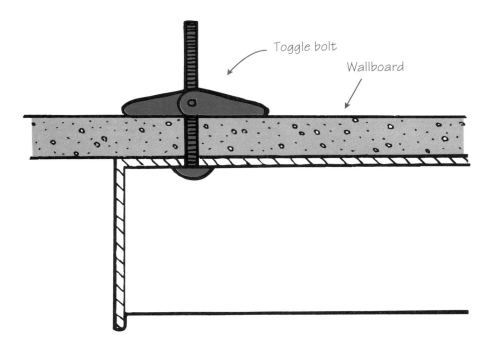

Toggle bolt

Wallboard

CHAPTER TEN

Using Central Heating & Cooling Systems Efficiently

Heating and cooling costs are a major part of the operating expenses of a home. Many factors affect the temperature in your home and the amount of energy consumed to achieve a comfortable level. The number of windows facing east and west, prevailing winds and landscaping, family size, the number of lights burning (about 90 per cent of the energy used by incandescent bulbs turns into heat), and the efficiency of your heating and cooling system all contribute to the temperature.

The ability of a system to heat or cool is measured in British thermal units, or Btus, per hour. A typical heating capacity, depending on the climate, can range from 80 thousand to 140 thousand Btus per hour. Cooling capacity might be measured in Btus or tons. In general, about 25 Btus per hour are needed to cool each square foot of floor space. A 2-ton air conditioner has a capacity of about 24 thousand Btus per hour. People often believe that larger is better when considering heating and cooling capacities, but oversized units are wasteful and inefficient. Heating is uneven: rooms tend to get too hot, then too cold. Air conditioners usually have an energy efficiency rating, or EER, stamped on the nameplate. This number represents the amount of Btus produced per watts of power. The higher the EER number, the more efficient the unit.

The simplest way to conserve energy is to adjust the thermostat. Turning your thermostat down 5 degrees before you leave for the day or go to bed can save from 14 to 25 percent of your total heating bill. Lower it another 3 degrees and you can save up to 35 percent, depending on the area of the country you live in. You can save about 10 percent on your cooling bill by turning your thermostat up 3 degrees in the summer. Replacing filters, adjusting dampers in room registers, checking the blower belt, and insulating the duct system are a few ways to improve the efficiency of your heating and cooling system.

Tools and Materials

- ❏ Screwdriver
- ❏ Adjustable wrench
- ❏ Vacuum with brush attachment
- ❏ Fin comb
- ❏ Needle-nose pliers
- ❏ Duct tape
- ❏ Utility knife
- ❏ Gloves
- ❏ Goggles
- ❏ Dust mask
- ❏ Insulation
- ❏ Filter
- ❏ Blower belt

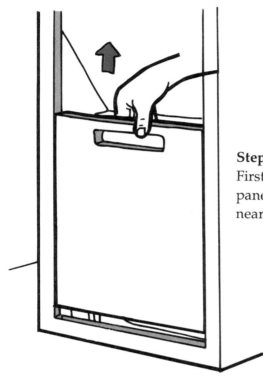

Step 10-1. Getting to the filter.
First turn off the thermostat. Remove the metal panel that covers the filter. The filter should be near the blower.

Step 10-2. Replacing the filter.
Slide the old filter out and install the new filter. Make sure the new filter is facing the right direction. Arrows indicating the direction of airflow are marked on the edge of the filter.

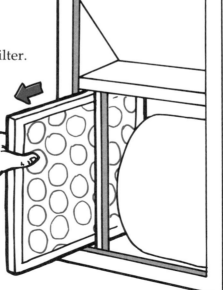

Step 10-3. Tightening the blower belt.

A loose blower belt can cause insufficient airflow. Turn off the breaker and remove the panel to the blower. Push down on the belt about halfway between the pulleys. It should give almost an inch if the tension is right. If the blower has a motor adjustment bolt, use a wrench to turn the bolt until the tension is correct.

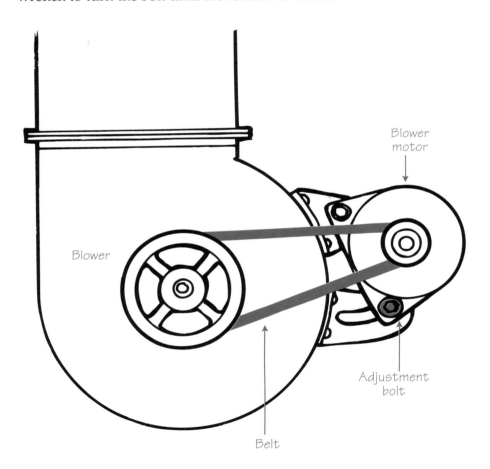

Blower

Blower motor

Adjustment bolt

Belt

Step 10-4. Replacing the belt.
If the blower has no adjustment bolt, and the belt needs replacing, work the belt over the lip of the motor pulley. Keep one hand on the belt while turning the pulley with the other. Take the old belt with you when you buy the new one. Install the new belt in the reverse order.

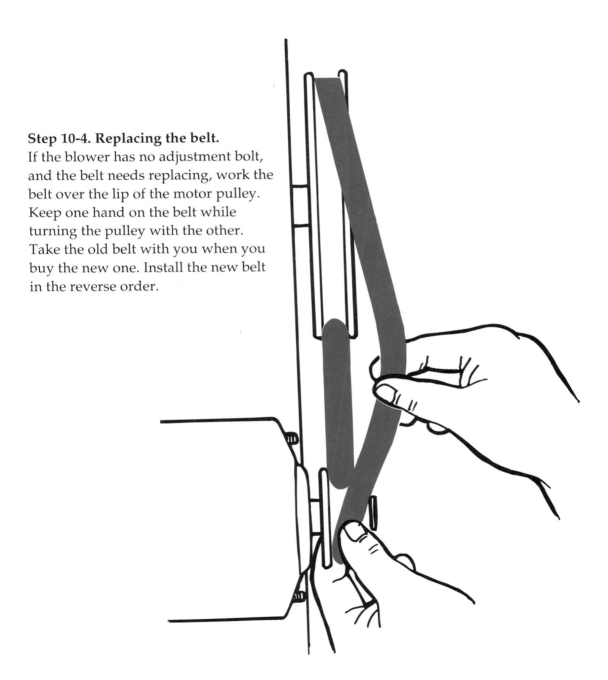

Step 10-5.
Adjusting the room temperature.
If you notice large differences in the temperatures between rooms, adjust the dampers in the room registers. Usually the damper controlling the airflow in the room farthest from the unit should be fully open, while the one in the room closest to the unit should be nearly closed.

Step 10-6.
Cleaning the filter on a window air conditioner.
First unplug the unit and remove the front cover. Now remove the filter. Some filters can be cleaned by vacuuming with a brush attachment and then washing with mild soap and water. Thoroughly rinse the filter and shake it dry.

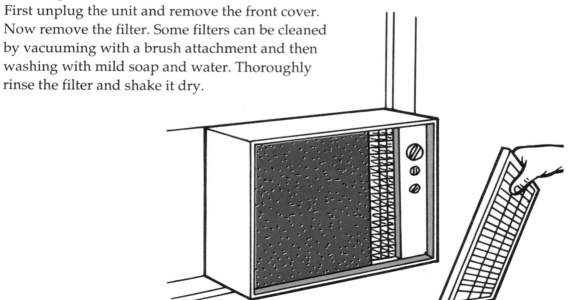

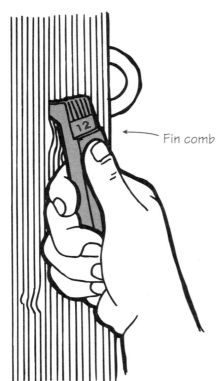

Fin comb

Step 10-7. Straightening the fins.

Behind the filter is the evaporator. Use the brush attachment and vacuum the fins. Straighten any bent fins with a fin comb. Don't use a knife or screwdriver—you might puncture the coils. Fin combs are sold in stores that sell refrigeration parts and in some building-supply stores. Make sure the spacing on the comb teeth matches the fins. Carefully fit the teeth between the fins in the undamaged section near the bent fins. Now pull the teeth through the damaged area, straightening the fins. Replace the filter and reinstall the panel.

Step 10-8.
Cleaning the outside air vents.

Remove any leaves or twigs with needle-nose pliers, being careful not to damage the fins behind the vents. These fins provide cooling for the condenser coil. If the fins are exposed, straighten any bent ones with the fin comb. Now plug the unit back in.

Step 10-9.
Servicing a central air conditioner.
First turn off the breaker in the service entrance panel, and turn off the disconnect switch near the unit. Now remove the top panel.

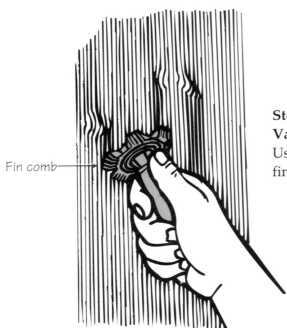

Fin comb

Step 10-10.
Vacuuming and straightening the fins.
Use the brush attachment to vacuum the coil fins. Straighten any bent fins with a fin comb.

Step 10-11.
Cleaning the fins.
Excess dirt can be removed by carefully spraying water through the fins from the inside out. Keep water away from the electrical contacts. Remember, combining water and electricity can be dangerous. Reinstall the top panel and turn the power back on.

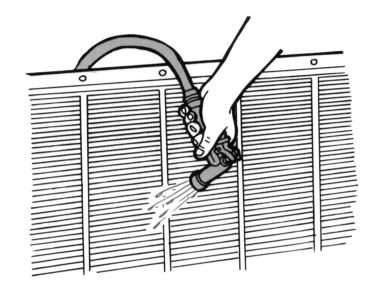

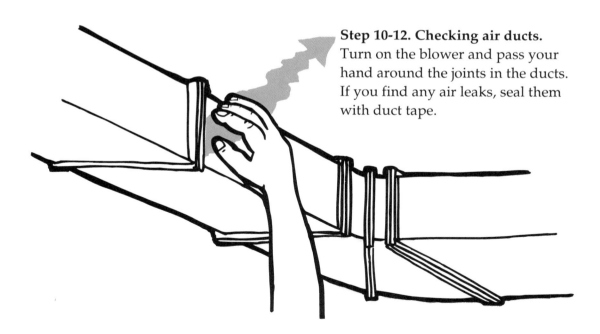

Step 10-12. Checking air ducts.
Turn on the blower and pass your hand around the joints in the ducts. If you find any air leaks, seal them with duct tape.

Step 10-13.
Wrapping ducts with insulation.
Insulate ducts with blankets or batts.
If the system is used for heating only,
the insulation might not have a vapor
barrier. However, if the ducts are
used for air conditioning as well as
heating, the insulation should have a
vapor barrier. Wrap the insulation
around the ducts with the vapor
barrier facing out. Try not to crush
the insulation, and keep it clear of
any chimneys and flue pipes.

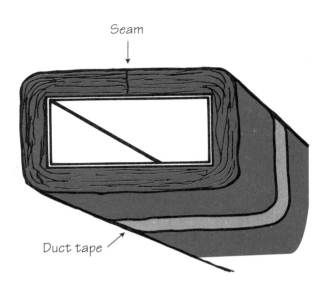

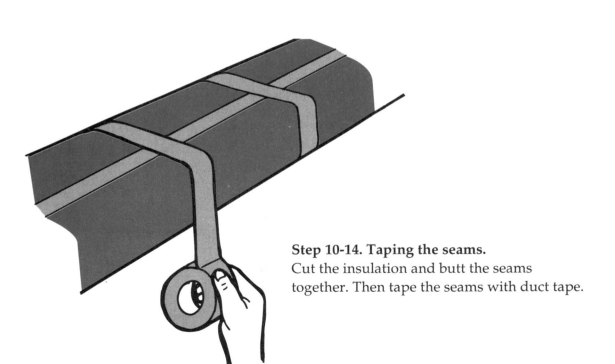

Step 10-14. Taping the seams.
Cut the insulation and butt the seams
together. Then tape the seams with duct tape.

Step 10-15. Covering the ends.
Cut the insulation so that you have two flaps
extending past the end of the duct. Fold
the flaps over the end of the duct
and fasten them in place
with tape.

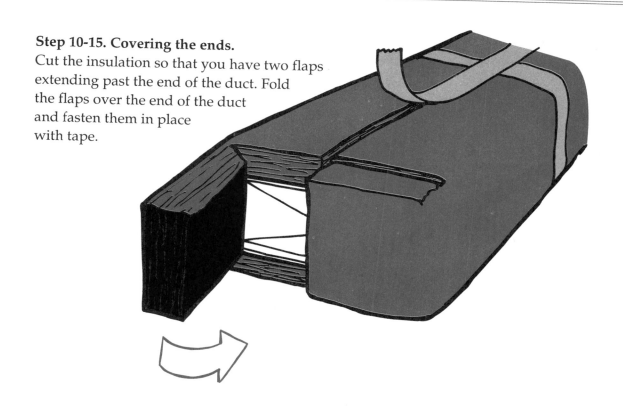

CHAPTER ELEVEN

Installing Ceiling Fans, Attic Fans, & Roof Turbines

When you are thinking about reducing air conditioning costs, understanding your comfort range is helpful. Generally, people feel comfortable when the temperature is between 72 and 78 degrees Fahrenheit, with the relative humidity between 35 and 60 percent. This range can be extended to 82 degrees with only a slight movement of air, about 2 mph.

A slow-turning ceiling fan can provide this amount of airflow easily. A whole-house attic fan can increase the comfort level throughout your home and satisfy your cooling needs on many days. If you install a turbine vent on your roof, the slightest breeze spins its blades, creating a slight low-pressure area inside the attic that actually pulls air through the attic.

Tools and Materials

- ❑ Voltage tester
- ❑ Screwdriver
- ❑ Wire stripper
- ❑ Wire nuts
- ❑ Utility knife
- ❑ Hand saw
- ❑ Hammer and nails
- ❑ Tape measure
- ❑ Saber saw
- ❑ Roofing cement
- ❑ Putty knife
- ❑ Caulking gun and caulking
- ❑ Adjustable wrench
- ❑ Ceiling fan, attic fan, or roof turbine

Ceiling fans are wired just like light fixtures. Some models are light enough to be installed on an existing metal outlet box, but heavier fans might need additional support. You can usually provide this additional support by attaching the outlet box directly to a wooden joist or a brace between the joists. You can use a threaded eye bolt to attach the fan to a wood member. Screw the bolt through an opening in the back of the box and into the wooden support. Remember not to place any strain on the wires.

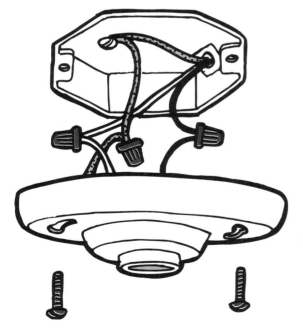

Step 11-1.
Preparing to install a ceiling fan.
Read the manufacturer's instructions carefully and thoroughly review any diagrams. Turn off the power to the circuit at the service entrance panel. Use the voltage tester to make sure the power is off, and then remove the existing fixture.

Step 11-2. Checking the outlet box.

You need to mount the fan to a standard 4-x-2⅛-inch metal octagon electrical box. The box must be firmly secured to a joist or reinforced to support the weight of the fan (at least 40 pounds). Do not use a plastic outlet box—it probably would not support the fan.

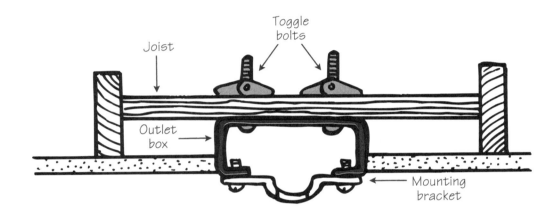

Step 11-3.

Installing the mounting bracket.
Securely fasten the mounting bracket to the outlet box, using the screws and washers provided with the fan. Make sure that the mounting bracket is securely tightened against the ceiling to keep the fan from wobbling.

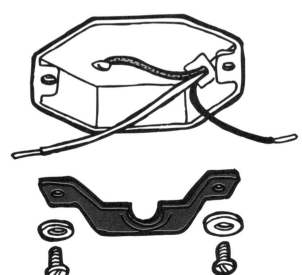

Step 11-4. Mounting the motor.

Lift the motor and downrod to the outlet box and fit the hang ball into the mounting bracket.

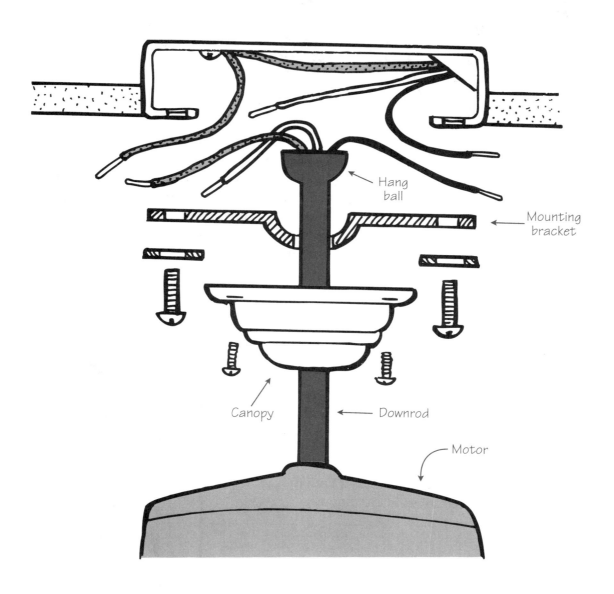

Hang ball

Mounting bracket

Canopy

Downrod

Motor

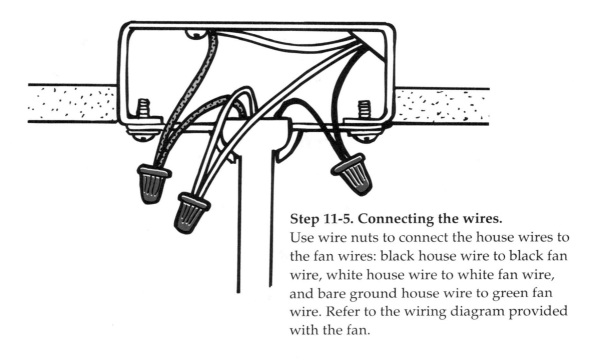

Step 11-5. Connecting the wires.
Use wire nuts to connect the house wires to the fan wires: black house wire to black fan wire, white house wire to white fan wire, and bare ground house wire to green fan wire. Refer to the wiring diagram provided with the fan.

Canopy

Step 11-6. Attaching the canopy.
Fold the wires up into the outlet box and slide the canopy up the downrod until it is flush with the ceiling. Tighten the setscrews in the canopy.

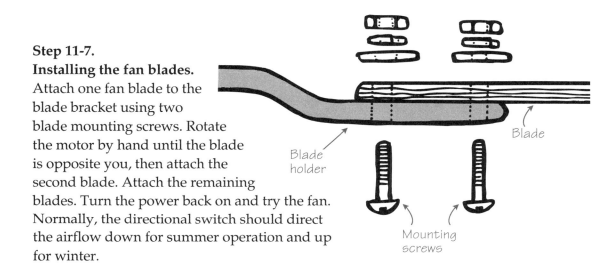

Step 11-7.
Installing the fan blades.
Attach one fan blade to the blade bracket using two blade mounting screws. Rotate the motor by hand until the blade is opposite you, then attach the second blade. Attach the remaining blades. Turn the power back on and try the fan. Normally, the directional switch should direct the airflow down for summer operation and up for winter.

A whole-house attic fan can be mounted in a hallway ceiling to suck air from the house and blow it into the attic. The attic must have sufficient outlet vents, and several windows in various areas of the house should be open.

Step 11-8.
Preparing to install a whole-house attic fan.
Select a suitable location for the fan, such as in a hallway ceiling. Check for any obstructions in the attic. Measure the size of the shutter to determine the size of the frame you will need in the ceiling. The inside dimensions of the frame should fit the opening in the shutter, allowing the shutter mounting screws to screw into the frame.

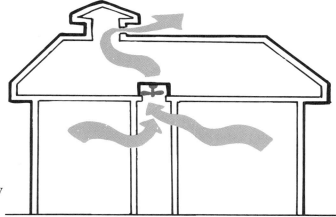

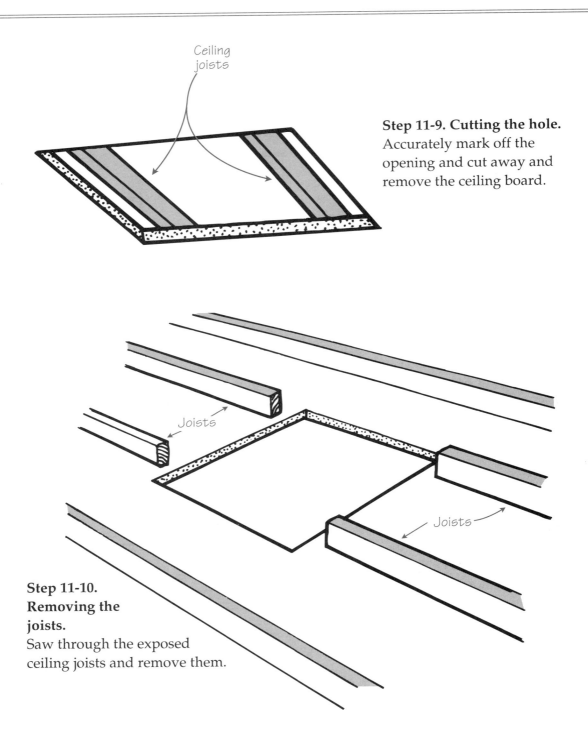

Ceiling joists

Step 11-9. Cutting the hole. Accurately mark off the opening and cut away and remove the ceiling board.

Joists

Joists

Step 11-10. Removing the joists. Saw through the exposed ceiling joists and remove them.

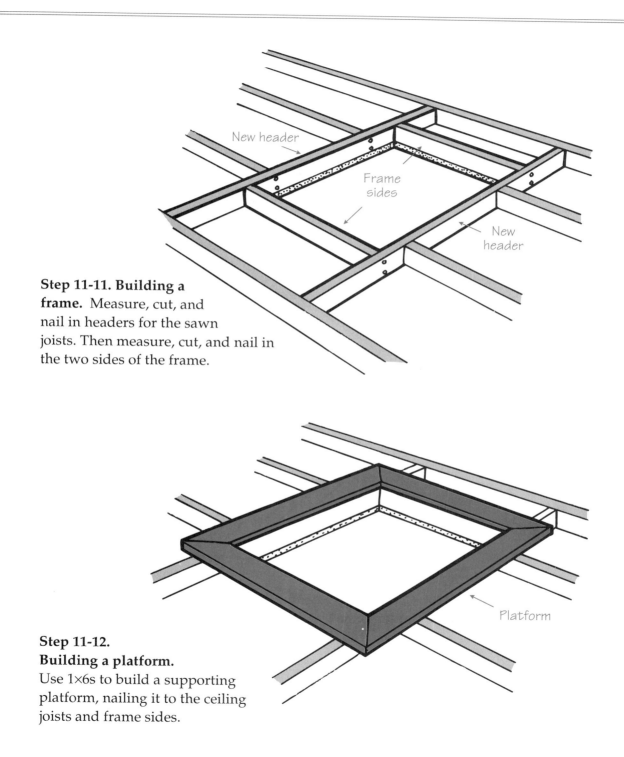

Step 11-11. Building a frame. Measure, cut, and nail in headers for the sawn joists. Then measure, cut, and nail in the two sides of the frame.

Step 11-12. Building a platform. Use 1×6s to build a supporting platform, nailing it to the ceiling joists and frame sides.

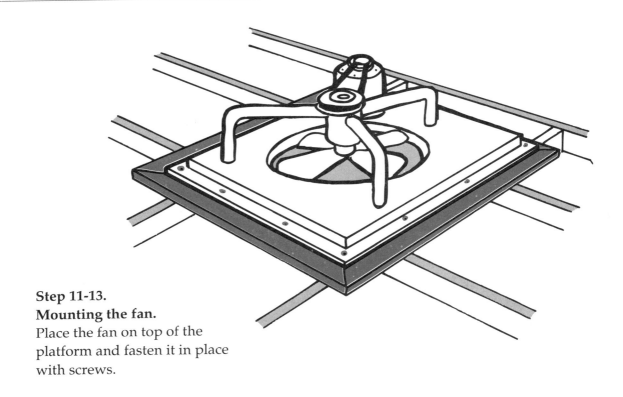

Step 11-13.
Mounting the fan.
Place the fan on top of the
platform and fasten it in place
with screws.

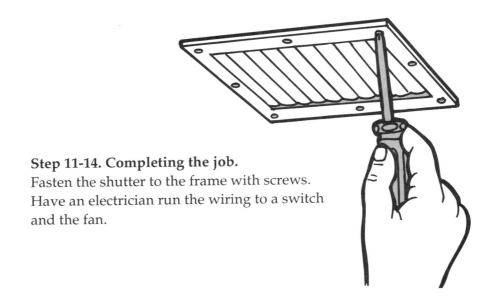

Step 11-14. Completing the job.
Fasten the shutter to the frame with screws.
Have an electrician run the wiring to a switch
and the fan.

Almost all homes have some type of attic venting in or near the roof, but it is usually not as much as it should be. A typical well-insulated attic should have about 1 square foot of ventilation for every 300 square feet of ceiling area. Common attic venting arrangements consist of vents under the eaves and gable vents at each end of the roof's peak. Ventilating the attic this way depends on the natural phenomenon of hot air rising and pulling cooler air in through the eaves vents while the hot air flows out the gable vents. A turbine vent installed on the roof works with the slightest breeze to enhance this process.

Step 11-15. Preparing to install a turbine vent.

Be sure to buy a vent that matches the pitch of your roof or is adjustable. From inside the attic, select a space centered between the rafters and drive a nail up through the roof to mark the location. Then, from on top of the roof, measure a hole the size of the vent base, centering the hole on the marking nail. Use a utility knife to cut the hole through the shingles and roofing felt.

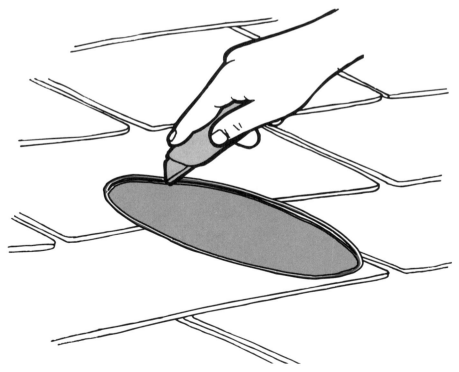

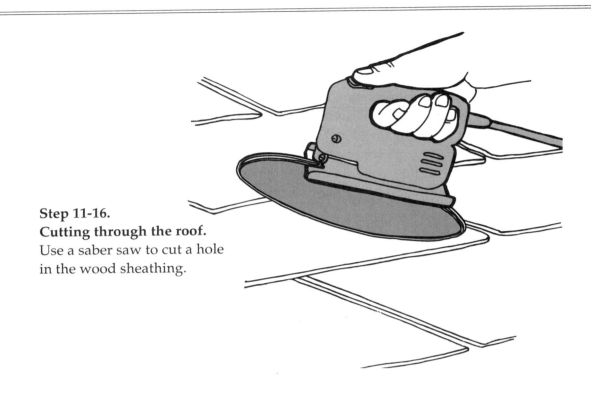

Step 11-16.
Cutting through the roof.
Use a saber saw to cut a hole
in the wood sheathing.

Step 11-17. Cementing the base.
Use a putty knife to apply roofing cement to
the bottom of the vent base flange. Slide the
flange under the shingles, centering the base
over the hole. If the base is adjustable, make
sure the top of the base is level.

Flange

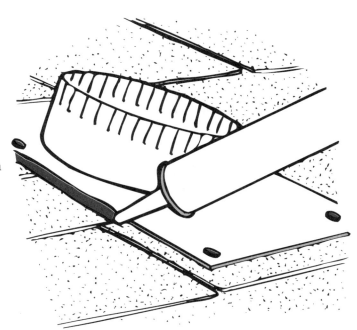

Step 11-18.
Securing the base.
Fasten the base in place with roofing nails, and caulk the edge of the flange and the nail heads.

Step 11-19. Completing the job.
Inside the turbine is a shaft. Place the end of the shaft in the supporting cup in the base. The other end of the shaft sticks up through the top of the turbine and fits into another cup on a bracket. The bracket is made up of three curved arms fitted around the turbine. Use the adjustable wrench to bolt the bracket to the base, positioning the shaft at the top of the turbine in the cup on the bracket. The turbine should be level and be free to turn in the slightest breeze.

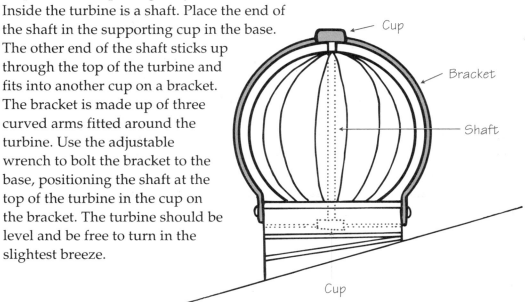

Cup

Bracket

Shaft

Cup

CHAPTER TWELVE

Using Major Appliances Efficiently

A typical household can save as much as 10 to 20 percent on energy costs by making small changes in the way it uses major appliances. These changes cost nothing and require no work. Refrigerators are one of the largest consumers of energy in the home. Today's models use about half as much energy as those produced 20 years ago. Better clothes dryers now have moisture sensors that turn the dryer off when the clothes are dry, saving about 15 percent on energy costs compared to a timed cycle. About 80 percent of the energy used by a dishwasher goes to heat the water. Many dishwashers have built-in heaters to raise the water temperature to about 140 degrees, the temperature recommended for the best cleaning, so you can turn down your home water heater and reduce energy costs. For every 10 degrees you lower the water heater's thermostat, you save about 5 percent in the energy used to heat water. Just by changing few cooking habits, you probably can save a lot of energy when preparing meals.

You can reduce the amount of energy your refrigerator uses by following the suggestions in Steps 12-1 through 12-6.

Step 12-1. Location.
Try to locate the refrigerator away from any source of heat such as a stove or dishwasher. Brush off or vacuum refrigerator coils about once a year.

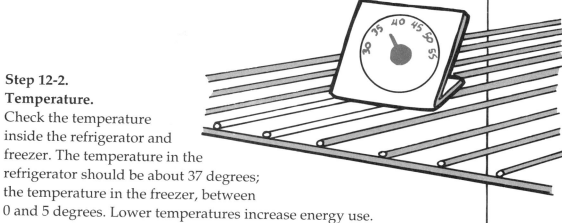

Step 12-2. Temperature.
Check the temperature inside the refrigerator and freezer. The temperature in the refrigerator should be about 37 degrees; the temperature in the freezer, between 0 and 5 degrees. Lower temperatures increase energy use.

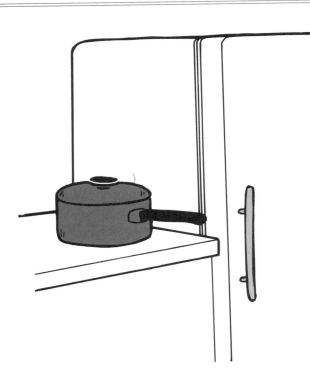

Step 12-3. Leftovers.
Cool hot foods before placing them
in the refrigerator or freezer.

Step 12-4. Humidity.
Cover foods, especially liquids, to keep them from releasing moisture
into the refrigerator. High humidity requires more energy to cool.

Step 12-5. Capacity.

Try to keep the refrigerator or freezer full. A full refrigerator operates more efficiently than a nearly empty one. You can freeze plastic containers of water to fill empty spaces in the freezer. Just don't cover any vents that send cold air to the refrigerator compartment, and leave a little space between items so air can circulate.

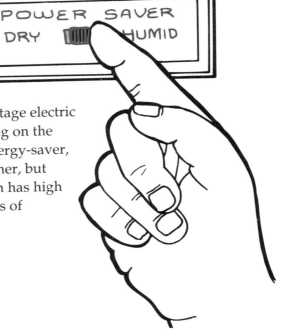

Step 12-6. Energy-saver switch.

The energy-saver switch controls a low-wattage electric heater that keeps condensation from forming on the outside of your refrigerator. Turn on the energy-saver, or power-saver, switch during humid weather, but leave it off during dry weather. If the switch has high and low settings, keep it on low unless areas of condensation form on your refrigerator.

Steps 12-7 through 12-14 suggest ways you can save energy and money while cooking.

Step 12-7. Gas stove.

When using a gas cooktop, adjust the flame so that it is slightly lower than, or just touches, the bottom of the pot. A flame that licks up the side of the pot wastes energy.

Step 12-8. Electric stove.

When using an electric cooktop, use a pot the same size or slightly larger than the element. A pot 2 inches smaller than the element can waste nearly 40 percent of the heat produced by the element. Use pots or pans with flat bottoms that have full contact with the element.

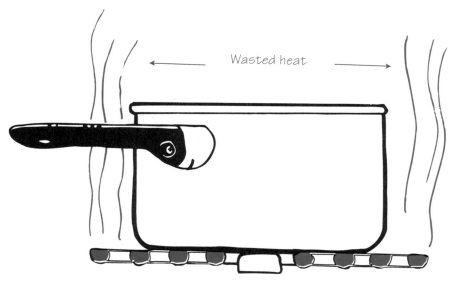

Wasted heat

Step 12-9. Pots and lids.

With either gas or electric cooking, use the smallest pot you can—it will require less energy to heat. Always use a lid. Some foods require about three times as much energy to cook without a lid on the pot.

Step 12-10. Drip pans.

Keep drip pans beneath the burners clean and shiny to reflect the heat up toward the pot. Blackened drip pans absorb heat and reduce the efficiency of the burner.

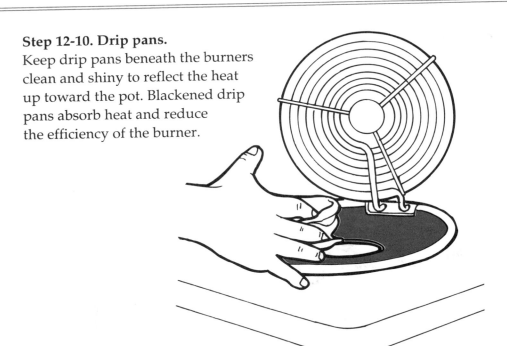

Step 12-11. Pressure cooker.

Pressure cookers use steam pressure to cook at a higher temperature, reducing cooking time by almost two-thirds and saving a considerable amount of energy. They are especially useful if you live at a high altitude.

Step 12-12. Self-cleaning oven.

Self-cleaning ovens use a tremendous amount of energy. Start the cleaning cycle while the oven is still warm from prior cooking, or, to save even more energy, clean the oven by hand. *Caution:* Before cleaning by hand or using any commercial oven cleaner on a self-cleaning oven, check the instruction manual for your oven.

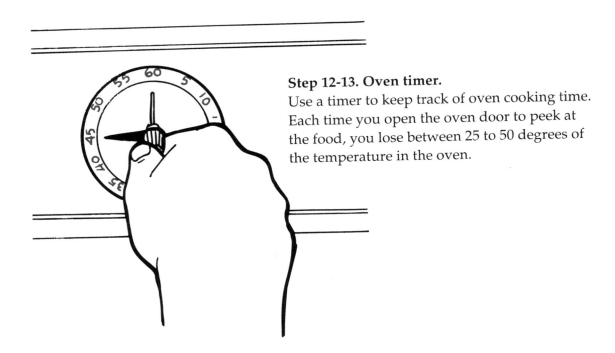

Step 12-13. Oven timer.
Use a timer to keep track of oven cooking time. Each time you open the oven door to peek at the food, you lose between 25 to 50 degrees of the temperature in the oven.

Step 12-14. Microwave oven.
Use a microwave oven to cook small- to medium-sized meals. You can save up to one-half the energy used by an electric oven. Cook larger quantities of food in the range oven.

Follow Steps 12-15 and 12-16 to save energy when you use your dishwasher.

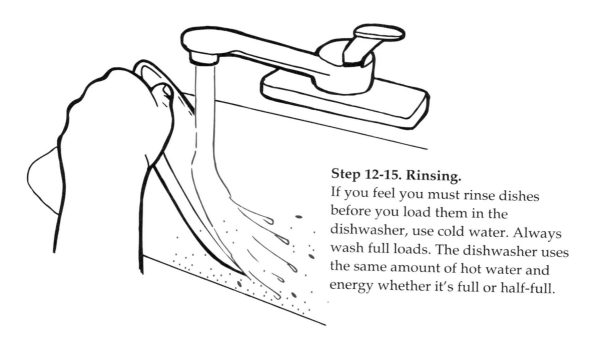

Step 12-15. Rinsing.
If you feel you must rinse dishes before you load them in the dishwasher, use cold water. Always wash full loads. The dishwasher uses the same amount of hot water and energy whether it's full or half-full.

Step 12-16. Drying.
Use the energy-saver switch if your machine has one, or, when the final rinse has finished, turn the control knob off, wait a minute for the steam to settle, then open the door, slide out the racks, and let the dishes air-dry.

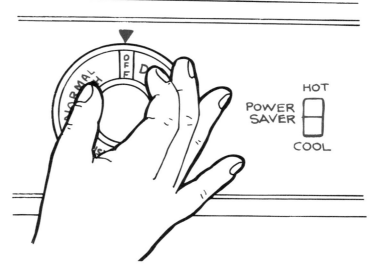

Steps 12-17 through 12-21 can help you save energy every time you do laundry.

Step 12-17. Water level and temperature.
Wash full loads or match the water level with the load. Use a warm or cold setting for the wash cycle instead of hot, and use cold water for the rinse cycle.

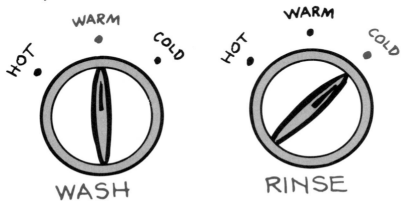

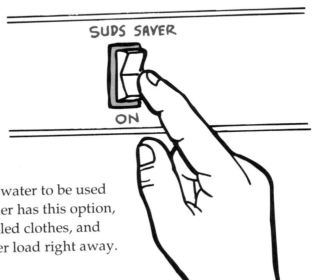

Step 12-18. Suds-saver switch.
A suds-saver option saves the wash water to be used again for the next load. If your washer has this option, use it only when washing lightly soiled clothes, and only if you are going to wash another load right away.

Step 12-19. Dryer loads.
When using the dryer, dry similar types of clothes together. Dry lighter fabrics separately from heavy fabrics. Dry full loads when possible. Drying small loads wastes energy, but so does overloading.

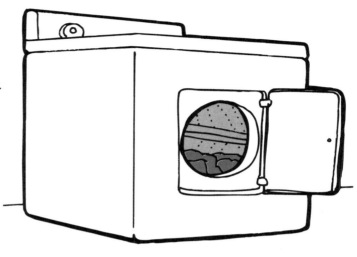

Step 12-20. Lint filter.
Clean the lint filter after every use. A clogged lint filter severely restricts the airflow and reduces the drying ability of the machine.

Step 12-21. Clothesline.
Use a clothesline when possible and let absolutely free wind and solar energy do the drying for you.

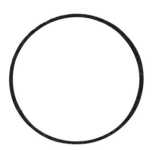

Glossary

ball cock
A valve in a toilet, operated by a lever
with a floating ball.

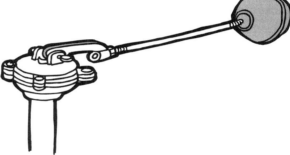

ball faucet
A single-lever faucet that uses a
hollow brass ball with holes to
control the flow of water.

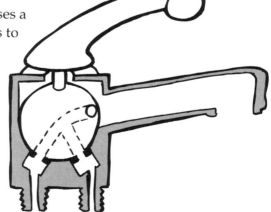

ball flush valve
A ball-shaped stopper in a toilet, used to release water from the tank to the bowl.

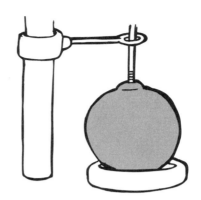

ceramic-disc cartridge
A cartridge, containing two ceramic discs, that controls the flow of water in one type of single-lever faucet.

eaves vent
Opening in the roof overhang that allows air to flow into the attic from outdoors.

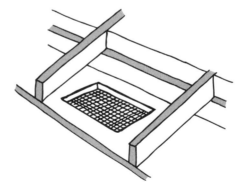

faucet seat
The tapered rim of the opening in a faucet that a washer presses against.

faucet seat dresser
A cutting tool used to smooth the surface of a faucet seat.

flapper flush valve
One kind of valve used in a toilet to release water from the tank to the bowl.

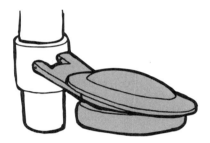

insulating batts
An insulating material 15 or 23 inches wide, precut in 4- or 8-foot lengths.

insulating blankets
Insulating material 15 or 23 inches wide that comes in rolls to be cut to length by the installer.

jumper wire
A short wire used to make electrical connections.

knockout
A partially cut opening in an
electrical box or fixture that
can be pressed out to allow
the passage of wires.

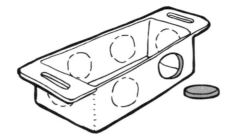

O-ring
A smooth, flexible ring, sometimes
rubber, used in a groove to create
a seal.

packing nut
A nut used to compress
the packing material around
a faucet stem.

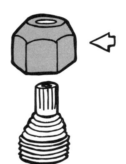

setscrew
A screw used to prevent movement
between parts.

shutoff valve
A valve used to control the flow
of water; usually fully opened
or closed.

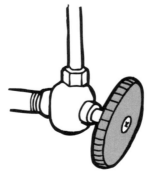

single-lever faucet
A faucet in which one handle regulates the temperature and the flow of water.

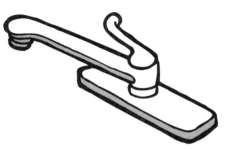

sleeve cartridge
A cartridge that has a movable sleeve with holes in it, used in one type of single-lever faucet to regulate the temperature and flow of water.

stem
The threaded part of a faucet that uses an O-ring and a washer to regulate the flow of water.

stem faucet
A faucet that uses a stem to regulate the flow of water.

vapor barrier
A thin layer or coating on insulation material, used to prevent the movement of moisture.

wire nut
A solderless connector used to join two or more electrical wires.

Index